Rubber
Stamp
Celebrations

From the rug on the floor to the border on the wall, and from the crib to the blocks, this miniature dollhouse room was brought to life simply by stamping. Even though exact instructions are not included in this publication, all techniques used in this room are found throughout this book, along with numerous other projects to decorate your home and your life.

Rubber Stamp Celebrations

Dazzling Projects from Personal Stamp Exchange

PERSONAL STAMP EXCHANGE

Sterling Publishing Co., Inc. New York
A Sterling/Chapelle Book

Personal Stamp Exchange:
Owner: Marina Golden

Design Team: Beth Clark, Cynthia Elmore, Saundra Farnsworth, Jeannene Chase Langford, Carol Santos, Stephanie Scheetz, Bev Smith, Samantha Starr, Monika Texeira

Additional Support: Barbara Fong, Stephanie Hartman, Tim Mancusi, and all others who have helped make this book possible.

Chapelle, Ltd.:
Owner: Jo Packham
Editor: Laura Best

Staff: Marie Barber, Ann Bear, Areta Bingham, Kass Burchett, Becky Christensen, Holly Fuller, Marilyn Goff, Shirley Heslop, Holly Hollingsworth, Sherry Hoppe, Shawn Hsu, Susan Jorgensen, Pauline Locke, Barbara Milburn, Linda Orton, Karmen Quinney, Leslie Ridenour, Cindy Stoeckl

Photographer: Kevin Dilley / Hazen Photography
Photo Stylists: Jo Packham, Peggy Bowers

Library of Congress–in–Publication Data

Rubber stamp celebrations ; dazzling projects from Personal Stamp Exchange.
     p. cm.
    Includes index.
    "A Sterling / Chapelle Book"
    ISBN 0-8069-6251-8
    1. Rubber stamp printing. I. Personal StampExchange (U.S.)
  TT867.R83   1998
  761—dc21   98-27255
                                CIP

A Sterling/Chapelle Book

10 9 8 7 6 5 4 3 2
First paperback edition published in 1999 by
Sterling Publishing Company, Inc.
387 Park Avenue South, New York, N.Y. 10016
Produced by Chapelle Ltd.
P.O. Box 9252, Newgate Station, Ogden, Utah 84409
© 1998 by Chapelle Ltd.
Distributed in Canada by Sterling Publishing
% Canadian Manda Group, One Atlantic Avenue, Suite 105
Toronto, Ontario, Canada M6K 3E7
Distributed in Great Britain and Europe by Cassell PLC
Wellington House, 125 Strand, London WC2R 0BB, England
Distributed in Australia by Capricorn Link (Australia) Pty Ltd.
P.O. Box 6651, Baulkham Hills, Business Centre,
NSW 2153, Australia

Printed and Bound in China
All rights reserved
Sterling ISBN 0-8069-6251-8 Trade
              0-8069-6291-7 Paper

If you have any questions or comments or would like information on specialty products featured in this book, please contact:
Chapelle, Ltd., Inc.
P.O. Box 9252, Ogden, UT 84409
(801) 621–2777 • (801) 621–2788 Fax

Every effort has been made to ensure that all information in this book is accurate. However, due to differing conditions, tools, and individual skills, the publisher cannot be responsible for any injuries, losses, and other damages which may result from the use of the information in this book.

Due to the limited amount of space available, we must print our patterns at a reduced size in order to give our patrons the maximum number of patterns possible in our publications. We believe the quality and quantity of our patterns will compensate for any inconvenience this may cause.

Personal Stamp Exchange

The PSX Art Department:
Monika Texeira, Beth Clark, Samantha Starr, Stephanie Scheetz, Saundra Farnsworth, Marina Golden,
Tim Mancusi, Cynthia Elmore, Carol Santos, Jeannene Chase Langford, Bev Smith

We are excited and very pleased to present you with this book whose pages hold hours of creative play and years of memories to come. Each of us brought our heart, talents, and discipline to this publication. We have all worked hard and drawn close together as we created and finessed these projects. This book is truly a result of people drawing the best from each other and holding each other up through the hours of hard work and rework.

Under the direction of Personal Stamp Exchange owner and artistic director, Marina Golden, our team brings you this exciting collection of stamp projects—stimulating ideas for every occasion. A wide array of techniques and materials have been used, ranging from the newest papers and mediums to favorite pieces of memorabilia, which we have collected over the years. Our hope is that this book will quicken your imagination and encourage you to create these projects, giving you the foundation to try other wonderful projects of your own.

Marina Golden has guided Personal Stamp Exchange for almost twenty years. Her design choices draw on her knowledge and appreciation of art and antiques, an affinity for early morning garden walks in search of the freshest of blooms, and the perspective of a true student and researcher—never satisfied until the facts are clear, whether the subject is an antique car, quilt designs of the Amish, or the exact colors of a Cedar Waxwing. Marina created and maintains the Personal Stamp Exchange look based on highly detailed, hand–drawn designs.

We know that as you turn the pages and see our exciting stamping ideas, that you will want to gather a collection of Personal Stamp Exchange collectable rubber stamps. This book is for you, create from your heart, explore the techniques, try on the colors, and let someone into your vision.

Table of Contents

January

February

March

July

August

September

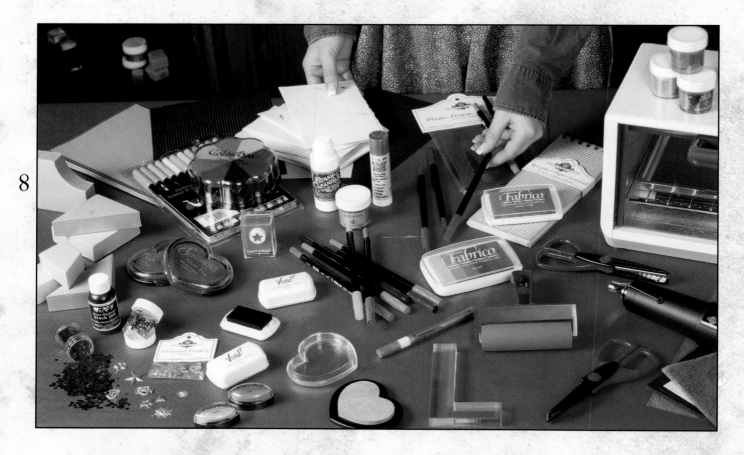

Shown above are some basic supplies needed for rubber stamping. Select a well lit area to set up a workspace. The work surface should be flat and sturdy. In addition to the basic supplies, have on hand: scissors, a craft knife, a self–healing cutting board, rulers, decorative hole punches, paintbrushes, assorted ribbons and trims, paper towels, and scrap paper.

Rubber Stamps

Rubber stamps are available in many sizes and are mounted on a wood block or on a piece of dense foam. The images are basically of two types—a stencil–type solid image, or a line drawing. A well–made stamp will give a detailed and clean impression when stamped, regardless of a wood or foam mount. Along with picture stamps, include some word stamps in your collection.

Inks

• **Dye ink pads** contain water–based, quick–drying inks that are available in a variety of colors. The felt pads are pre–inked and housed in a plastic container. Raised dye ink pads are suitable for use with any size stamp because the felt pad is raised beyond the rim of the plastic container. Dye inks may be used for stamping on all papers, but colors may bleed slightly on absorbent, uncoated papers. Dye ink is not fade–resistant.

• **Embossing ink pads** contain slow–drying, colorless, or lightly tinted, water–based inks form-ulated to be used with colored embossing powders. The initial application of ink can be applied from the bottle to a new dry pad, then re–inked as needed. Some embossing pads are pre–inked.

• **Fabric, permanent, or multipurpose ink pads** contain water– or solvent–based inks that are suitable for stamping on a variety of surfaces and may or may not require heat–setting. When the ink is dry or set, images can be colored with water–based ink pens, paints, or watercolor pencils without colors bleeding. Some multipurpose inks may be slow–drying enough to be embossed.

• **Home decorating inks** are solvent–based inks available in many colors, including copper, gold, and silver. These inks are opaque, quick–drying, and can be used on ceramic, fabric, glass, metal, paper,

plastic, and wood. The ink is suitable for stamping decorative objects for the home. Washing is not recommended.

• **Metallic ink pads** can be water–soluble, acid–free, and nontoxic inks, offering a brilliant shine without embossing. Check product label for qualities.

• **Pigment ink pads** contain thick, slow–drying inks in a sponge pad, suited for use with clear embossing powders. Pigment ink pads are available in vivid, fade–resistant colors. Because the sponge pad sits on top of the plastic container bed, it is perfect for inking any size stamp.

• **Rainbow ink pads** contain side–by–side felt or foam cushions of different colored inks set together on one ink pad. Pads are available with either dye or pigment ink.

• **Re–inkers** are bottles of dye, pigment, or embossing inks used to refresh ink on dry pads.

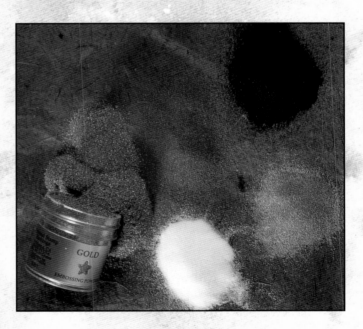

Embossing Powders

Embossing powders are used to coat, seal, and raise an image that has been stamped with a slow–drying ink. The powder is applied and heated to its melting point, creating a raised image. The heating also fuses powder to ink and adheres both to the stamped surface.

9

• **Clear embossing powders** are transparent powders used to coat an image stamped with slow–drying ink. The ink is usually colored. After heating, the embossed stamped image will retain the color of the ink used in the stamping. Clear powders mixed with semitransparent powders, iridescent powders, or finely ground glitters, make interesting blends of clear–based embossing powders. These also are best used over colored pigment inks or other slow–drying colored inks.

10

• **Colored embossing powders** are opaque powders with color, including metallics, such as copper, gold, and silver. To maintain the true colors of these powders, they should be used with clear or lightly tinted embossing inks.

Embossing Heat Sources

Embossing heat sources adhere powder to projects with a melting heat, as opposed to a drying heat. The most convenient and efficient tool is a heat gun which provides the necessary degree of melting heat for the powder to emboss. Because the tool is hand–held, heat can be directed to the top of the stamped surface. Care must be taken when embossing over painted surfaces, as the intensity of heat could cause paint to blister. Other sources of melting heat are radiating heat from an electric burner, toaster, iron, or light bulb. A hair dryer gives off a drying heat that is not hot enough to emboss.

Stamping Surfaces

Stamping surfaces include paper, fabric, wood, glass, and even candles. Projects throughout this book use a variety of surfaces. When projects call for cardstock (8½ x 11" sheet), blank cards (recipe cards or postcards), vellum (8½ x 11" sheet), or tissue paper (sheet) it is the crafter's choice as to the completed size.

Ribbon should be premeasured around project for amount needed. Ornaments such as porcelain, porcelain bisque and iridescents can be purchased in crafter's desired size.

When stamping on a new or unfamiliar surface, practice on a piece of scrap paper or underside of project before working on actual.

The most common material used for stamping is paper, and there is a wide range of papers suitable for stamping. Aside from smooth or lightly textured cardstock, paper as thin and delicate as tissue or as thick as cardboard can be used. Some papers are more absorbent than others, which will affect the ink used. Experiment with embossing on various types of paper. Some will prove to be more compatible than others with the embossing powders and heating technique.

Papers that do not work for direct stamping can be used as backing papers. Big sheets or rolls of blank paper can be stamped on to make wrapping paper.

• **Watercolor pencils** give a similar result when the pencil color is diluted with a bit of water from a paintbrush. Also consider watercolor paints, chalks, and colored pencils for adding color to stamped images on paper. To apply color to other surfaces, try fabric pens and acrylic or porcelain paints.

Markers, Pens & Pencils

• **Art markers** make a dramatic effect that can be attained by diluting the pen colors with a little water from a paintbrush. The image is stamped on paper; color is added, then blended by diluting with water. Pen colors can also be blended on a palette with water before applying to the stamped design.

• **Embossing pens** have a slow–drying ink that remains wet long enough to be embossed. The ink colors can be blended on paper before being embossed with clear powder. Also available is a colorless ink embossing pen for writing or highlighting designs to be embossed with any embossing powder.

• **Fabric ink pens** are perfect for applying permanent color to fabrics. The colors can be blended and do not need to be heat–set.

• **Water–based ink pens** are generally used to apply color to stamped designs. Some of these inks are translucent, others more opaque, but both are suitable for coloring stamped images on paper. The translucent colors lend themselves to blending, while the denser colors work especially well for coloring directly on the rubber before stamping. Water–based pens are available in a wide color range and some have dual tips—a brush tip for coloring and a writing tip. The inks in these pens are not fade resistant.

Adhesives

• **Double–sided tape, permanent tape adhesive, and glue sticks** are just a few of the many adhesives that work well to attach light– to medium–weight papers together. Any clear liquid glue should be used sparingly, as the paper will buckle if too wet.

• **Glue pens** are handy for adhering lightweight papers or for embossing. Glue pens create a permanent bond when glue is used wet, and a temporary bond when glue is allowed to dry before affixing.

• **Spray adhesive** is ideal for providing a smooth, seamless bond. It is suitable for use with most weights and thicknesses of paper.

• **Temporary adhesive** is useful where a permanent bond is not desired, as on an envelope flap, or holding a stamping mask to paper.

12

Stamp Positioners

Stamp positioners are helpful for indicating exactly where to stamp on a project. There are many styles available. Though they vary slightly from brand to brand, the applications are similar; follow manufacturer's instructions.

Stamp Cleaners

Stamp cleaners are a cleaning solution specially formulated to remove ink from the rubber surface of the stamp, and will not harm rubber, foam,

adhesive, or wood on the stamp. Clean stamp when changing ink types or colors by following manufacturer's instructions.

Several stamp cleaning solutions are available. Clean solvent–based inks with appropriate cleaner. Use a soft bristle brush to help remove any buildup of dried ink on the rubber.

Archival & Acid–free Materials

Archival & acid–free materials consist of pH–neutral and archival inks, powders, and papers: Due to environmental and photo keepsake longevity concerns, the acid–free properties of stamping accessories have become especially important. Stampers have increasingly become aware of the archival quality of the papers used in their projects.

The pH of paper is determined by the amount of alkaline in the paper. It is measured on a scale of 1 to 14. A lower number indicates greater acidity, which over time has a corrosive effect on papers containing high levels of it, and materials touching those papers. Acid–free papers have a pH level of at least 6.5. The standards of archival materials are set by government agencies. Archival paper must have a pH of 7.5 to 8:5 and include 2% calcium carbonate.

Inks are also tested for acid levels. Pigment inks are considered acid–free/neutral, while dye inks are not. Embossing powders are considered pH–neutral.

Stamping Techniques

The following basic stamping techniques are used in making the projects in this book.

Inking, Stamping & Cleaning

Inking, stamping, and cleaning the stamp correctly is important to create a good impression. The pad should be clean and evenly inked before beginning. In most cases, if pad is dry, a re–inker can be used to re–ink pad. Add ink to pad a few drops at a time, then work ink into pad, using paper towels or tip of re–inker bottle, until ink is evenly absorbed by pad.

To ink stamp, lightly tap stamp a few times on top of pad. There is no need to push or scrub stamp back and forth over pad. After tapping a few times, turn stamp over to check the amount of ink on the rubber. If it looks well inked, stamp is ready to use.

Stamp on scrap paper first to check image and get the "feel" of the stamp. Holding stamp firmly, press down on paper, taking care not to rock or move stamp. When using a larger stamp, it may be easier to stand up while stamping, creating more pressure. Carefully pressing on each corner also helps to assure a completely stamped image. To remove stamp, carefully lift straight up in one motion. When a successful image is achieved on scrap paper, stamp can be re–inked and stamped on project.

After stamping or before changing to a new color, it is important to clean stamp. Bottled stamp cleaner is easy to use and comes formulated to remove general, as well as specific inks from rubber. To use cleaner, lightly rub applicator over rubber, then wipe dry with paper towels. If stamp is cleaned immediately, ink is easier to remove. Some more permanent inks are harder to remove and may need a second cleaning.

14

Blending

Blending is the mixing of two or more colors. It gives a design a more realistic or dimensional look. In many cases, softening the colors can be done by using a blender pen, or by simply coloring one color over another until a different shade is achieved. While blending colors on paper, it is important not to overwork the paper, as it may tear.

Watercoloring

Watercoloring can be used to blend and soften colors. This technique involves thinning one color or blending two or more colors together, using a paintbrush loaded with water. Sometimes it is

helpful to apply marker colors onto a palette or waxed paper, using a wet paintbrush. Add water to thin colors to the desired shades. Creating a wash, using the watercoloring technique, also works well for adding color to the background of stamped projects.

Coloring & Painting on the Stamp

Coloring and painting on the stamp can be done with water–based markers, resulting in an image that is multicolored when stamped. Color from light to dark, especially if blending colors. If color has dried, exhale on stamp to remoisten ink before stamping.

This technique can also be used when color is desired on only selected parts of an image. Simply color specific lines or sections. The uninked lines will not stamp. (Make certain the entire stamp is clean before starting.)

When applying paint directly onto the rubber, make certain to test painted stamp on scrap paper first, as paint may need to be thinned to get a clear, crisp image. Paint can be brushed or "dabbed" on, using a sponge brush. Clean stamp often when stamping many times, as paint tends to thicken and fill in grooves of the rubber.

Embossing transforms ink on a flat stamped image into a dimensional image by fusing finely grained clear or colored powders to stamped ink.

1 Embossing
Ink stamp, then press on surface to be decorated.

2 Pour embossing powder on wet ink. Shake off excess. A dry, fine paintbrush can be used to dust off any unwanted powder.

3 Heat powder until it melts. A heat gun is a good heat source to melt powder, as it works well to heat all surfaces.

There are many kinds and colors of powders available. In general, colored powders, including metallics and tinsels, work best if used over embossing ink, while clear–based powders are used over colored inks. For a unique look, try pouring more than one powder over wet ink, or experimenting with different colored inks under the powders.

In addition, powdered pigment can be used in various ways to add a lustrous depth to the surface of a stamped project. Powdered pigment can be rubbed or brushed over the surface or over an embossed design. It can also be mixed into just about any medium, including embossing powders, clays, paints, varnish, and more, then applied accordingly. If powder is not baked–on or dried into the design, then it must be sealed with a varnish medium or similar sealer fixature to make color permanent.

Water embossing adds dimension to a design by adding water to paper so sections "puff out." There are two different methods to emboss with water. Both methods work best on paper with a high cotton or rag content, such as recycled or cotton handmade paper.

16

1 **Water Embossing—Method 1**
Apply water on an already stamped card, using a paintbrush and allow it to soak in.

3 Press image gently with fingertips from reverse side to complete the puffed–out look.

2 Place image right side up on a soft surface. Push paper in until desired effect is achieved, using the small, rounded point of a burnisher or the handle tip of a paintbrush.

1 **Water Embossing—Method 2**
Wet a blank piece of paper on both sides by brushing it with water where image will appear.

2 Place stamp on work surface, rubber side up. Place paper upside down on top of rubber stamp and use a burnisher to mold paper into and around stamp image. As paper begins to stretch overall, more pressure may be applied until designed degree of relief is achieved.

3 Carefully lift paper off stamp. If a tear or hole is created, repair by "meshing" pieces together and smoothing with water. When paper dries, the tear will be mended. When selecting a stamp, remember: small areas are difficult to work with; while puffing out too large of an area will weaken paper.

Paper Layering & Collaging

Paper layering and collaging help frame the stamped image and draw the eye into the picture. It can also be used to draw attention to an important design element. While it is simple to do, some thought and planning should go into the color, paper choice, and placement of the piece. (See Theme, Color & Design on pages 30–32.)

When layering papers, it is important to experiment with different textures and colors until the desired look is achieved. Sometimes it is helpful to use a temporary adhesive to hold down layers while trying different arrangements. Papers can be ripped, torn, crinkled, or cut with regular or decorative scissors. One layer or many can be added.

When working with different paper thicknesses and textures, it is important to select the proper adhesive. Thin or sheer papers require a light adhesive, such as a spray adhesive, so glue does not show through. Heavier papers, require a thicker, stronger glue, such as a white craft glue. When securing trinkets or other bulkier findings, an industrial–strength adhesive is a good choice.

Masking allows stamped images to appear behind other images. This technique is useful when brayering or sponging the background. See Brayering on page 25 or Sponging on page 26 for more information.

18

1 **Masking**
Stamp an image onto desired surface, then another onto self–adhesive notepaper. Cut out notepaper image and place over first image.

3 Align a stamp positioner when masking to assure proper alignment of images.

2 Stamp another image, overlapping the covered one. When notepaper is removed, the second image will appear to be behind the first. (Instead of self–adhesive notepaper, any type of thin paper and double–sided, removable tape can be used.)

4 Completed masking images.

Stamping on Wood

Stamping on wood requires a sanded, smooth stamping surface. Unfinished wood should be sealed or painted to prevent ink from bleeding into wood. Once dry, wood should be sanded again with a fine–grade sandpaper, then wiped with a clean, soft cloth.

While most inks and paints work well on wood, a permanent, multipurpose stamping ink works best to produce a clear, crisp image. Stamped images can be colored with art brush pens, fabric markers, or paint, if desired. Sealing the finished project with a spray or brush–on sealer is recommended, especially if project will be handled.

Stamping on Fabric

Stamping on fabric is possible, using any number of inks and paints available for stamping on fabric. Some require heat–setting while others will set by air–drying. Always read manufacturer's instructions before stamping. Carefully consider properties and treatment of fabric. A paint that needs to be heat–set would not be a good choice for fabric that should not be heated. There are certain types of fabrics that work best for stamping, such as polished cottons, moiré, silk, sheeting, canvas, and other materials with a tight weave. Fabrics to avoid include loose and stretchy weaves and furry or nubby materials, such as felts and flannels.

As with all stamping projects, it is important to test stamp on a scrap of fabric to see how ink/paint will react. The image may look good when stamped, but may fade after washing. Also, by testing, one can get a better feel for how ink will "sit" on fabric. The ink may bleed or run, causing image to blur.

Be certain to prewash fabric to remove sizing, especially if item will be worn. Do not use a fabric softener as it may coat material with a stain guard, preventing a successful stamping. To make stamping on fabric easier, secure fabric to cardboard or stretch it over a frame. Waxed paper can be ironed on the back, or clear shelf paper adhesive can be applied to keep fabric from stretching while keeping project cleaner and neater.

Stamping on velvet produces a beautiful shimmery imprint that contrasts against the nap of velvet. Once the stamp design is set into the velvet, the material can be used in just about any fabric project.

20

1 Stamping on Velvet
Place stamp, rubber side up. Lightly mist right side of velvet with water. Lay velvet right side down on stamp. The stamp can also be inked before ironing. Lightly ink stamp with textile paint. Quickly place dry velvet over stamp, then iron.

3 Carefully lift iron and remove velvet. Spraying with water is not recommended when using ink.

Stamping on glass, ceramics, and porcelain can be done with multipurpose ink, then painted.

2 Position iron so steam holes will not overlap design. Using wool setting without steam, press iron over wrong side of velvet for approximately 20 seconds. Do not move iron.

1 Stamping on Glass, Ceramics & Porcelain
Ink stamp with a multipurpose ink, then gently set stamp on scrap paper to remove excess ink.

2 Stamp directly on project surface, or set inked stamp, rubber side up, on table and press surface of project on stamp.

Stamping on Candles

   Stamping on candles is a little tricky because the surface is not as smooth as it looks. With practice, it becomes easier. On some types of candles, rubbing alcohol can be used to wipe away mistakes.

   Ink stamp with a home decorating ink. Gently set stamp on scrap paper to remove excess ink. Carefully pick up stamp and press it onto candle's surface. If working with a round, pillar candle, it is easier to place stamp, rubber side up, on work surface and quickly roll candle across stamp. Check image on candle; if some of the design is missing, a small paintbrush with some ink can be used to touch it up. The stamped design can be painted with porcelain paints or home decor ink; embellished with ribbon, glitter glue, or dimensional paint; or left plain.

3 Paint stamped image with porcelain paint, to add color. Follow manufacturer's instructions, as many paints require oven baking.

   If a mistake is made, most can be wiped off with baby wipes before it dries, or scraped off with a razor blade after they dry. Mistakes on nonglossy or porous surfaces, such as terra cotta or bisque, will not come off because ink is absorbed into material.

Working with modeling compounds can create a project or produce a mold for other uses. A variety of modeling compounds, commonly called clay, are available and lend themselves well to stamping. Read the manufacturer's instructions. Some compounds need to be baked, while others air–dry overnight.

1 Working with Modeling Compounds
Roll clay out into a thin slab. Press stamp into soft material.

3 Paint or color design with paints or inks. Spray or brush a sealer onto the finished piece to help protect the design.

2 Cut out stamp impression, using a stylus, and smooth edges. Dry or bake according to manufacturer's instructions.

4 Recess or reverse impression, if desired, by making a mold from modeling compounds, following steps 1 and 2.

5 Roll out clay on a smooth surface into a thin slab.

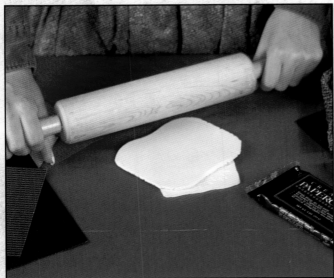

6 Place thin slab of clay on top of mold. Press clay into grooves of mold, using a rolling pin. A mold release is recommended for easy removal. Clear embossing ink/pad, when pressed/rubbed onto mold will effectively work as a mold release agent.

7 Carefully lift clay from mold, then trim, smooth, and leave to dry. This mold technique works best with bold designs and is not appropriate for designs with words or letters, as image will be reversed.

8 Paint or color design with paints or inks. Spray or brush a sealer on the finished piece to help protect design.

Finishes, Forms & Findings

Backgrounds traditionally are used to unify, accent, orient, and embellish stamp art, creating an overall finished look. Most craft stores carry an assortment of finishes that also may be used with stamps to develop interesting backgrounds. Faux finishes, such as crackle, woodgraining, antiquing, and marbling, are available. Always read and follow the manufacturer's instructions. There are also a wide variety of embossing powders that provide different colors and textures for your stamped art.

Beautiful and elegant backgrounds may be created by simply sponging color onto stamping surfaces. This technique blends and softens colors, giving depth and movement to the surface. Experiment with different sponges, such as cosmetic, sea, or bath sponges, to achieve a variety textures.

Embellishing

Embellishing and special touches may be used to enhance cards, gifts, and other projects.

This can be as easy as gluing special findings to the piece. Items, such as ribbon scraps, trinkets, beads, feathers, and other treasures, often add special meaning or a personal touch. Keep a special box to house a collection of findings and be certain to use the appropriate adhesives.

Other craft accessories that accent projects include glitter glues and pearlized liquids. These decorative liquids are squeezed onto the surface and left to air–dry. Depending upon the desired look, sparkling glitter, pearl drops, faux appliqué, and other textures can be used to create a special touch.

Brayering softens colors used in a background. Brayering spreads colors evenly over a surface, especially over a large area, and is good for applying color gradations.

1 Brayering
Roll brayer over a stamp pad of single or multiple colors. Roll colored brayer over project.

3 Ink stamp and apply over brayered pattern on project.

2 Re-ink brayer and again roll over project next to first application.

Découpaging is decorating a surface with cut or torn pieces of paper that are glued to the project with a clear liquid adhesive. This technique is especially useful when stamping on a project that is uneven. This procedure also allows the use of word stamps on a glass surface.

1 Découpaging
Stamp pieces of paper with ink or emboss, and color images.

3 Apply more découpage medium, varnish, or spray sealer.

2 Brush surface with découpage medium. Lay paper pieces on wet surface and brush with découpage medium. Let dry.

Sponging
Sponging blends coloring into an elegant background. Apply paint or ink to a sponge and dab color onto project. Add one color over another, until desired effect is achieved.

Making a bag is as easy as wrapping a present. A sheet of paper, tape or glue, and a book or box for use as a mold is all that is needed. Be certain paper is long enough to wrap around mold, with an extra inch for overlapping. Bags can be used for a number of things, from holding special gifts and treats, to housing the luminous glow of a votive.

1 Making a Bag
Stamp and embellish paper as desired. Let dry. Wrap paper around mold, overlapping edges at back; tape.

2 Fold bottom flaps and secure them with tape, just like wrapping one end of a gift. Carefully slide mold out top and fold sides of bag in, creasing them in half at top.

3 Punch holes at top of bag on each side and thread them with cord or ribbon if handles are desired.

Making a box for special occasions can be easy. A box can be stamped with a number of Pixie Stamps™ or Teeny Weenys™. Stamp boxes in festive colors and fill with little toys and candy for party favors, or use gold ink and tie with a white bow for elegant wedding favors.

Making a Box

1. Lightly trace lines from specific box pattern onto back of cardstock or paper, using transfer paper and a sharp pencil.

2. Carefully cut out the shape, using scissors or a craft knife and a metal ruler. Lightly score and crease all of the fold lines to make paper easier to fold.

3. Turn paper over; stamp and decorate. Add glitter, markers, or other stamping accessories for more enhancement. Let dry.

4. Assemble box according to specific box instructions.

Small & Large Pillow Box Instructions

1. Complete Making a Box steps.

2. Fold on center score, apply glue to the outside of the tab and press it to the inside of the box (making a cylinder.) Hold together until glue adheres. Fold in end flaps on each side.

Large Pillow Box Pattern

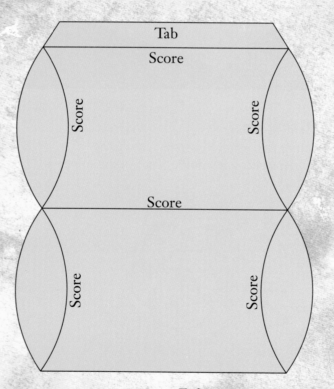

Small Pillow Box Pattern

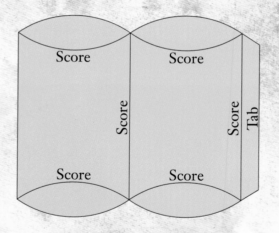

Enlarge patterns 165%

28

Cube Box Pattern

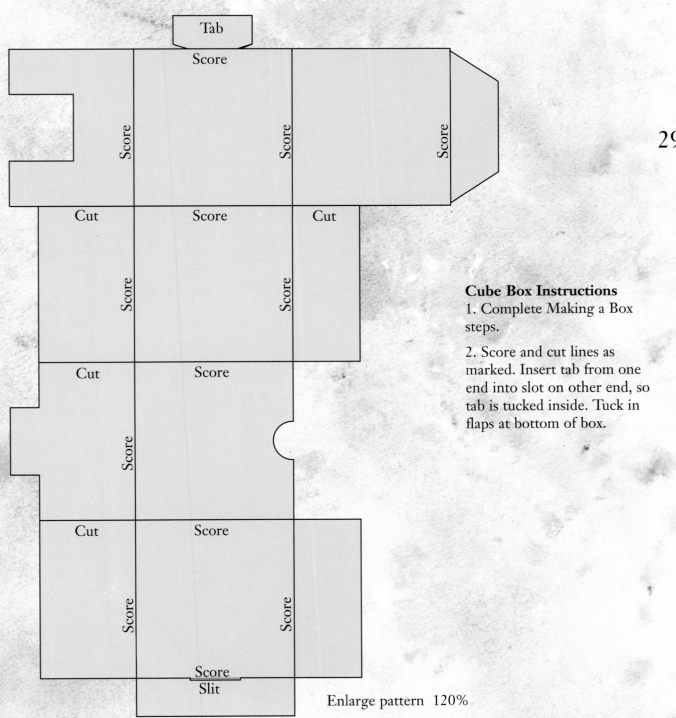

29

Cube Box Instructions

1. Complete Making a Box steps.

2. Score and cut lines as marked. Insert tab from one end into slot on other end, so tab is tucked inside. Tuck in flaps at bottom of box.

Enlarge pattern 120%

Theme

What stamps will you use? Every stamping project requires a theme or subject. If you decide to create a card, invitations, or wrapping paper for a specific occasion, certain stamp designs will automatically come to mind. A cake with candles and greeting for a birthday card, booties and an RSVP stamp for a baby shower invitation, or a scary jack–o–lantern and black cats for a Halloween treat bag might be obvious choices for those events. Florals and other natural elements, like leaves and shells are suitable for numerous occasions. Part of the joy of stamping is being able to customize your creations by choosing from the extensive selection of stamp designs available. Focus on special interests of the recipient and add touches of your own personality.

Focus on special interests of the recipient and add touches of your own personality.

30

Allow yourself to experiment with variations on basic themes. Designs that seem limited to a particular holiday may be used in a different context during the same season. If a baby shower will take place during Christmas, it might be fun to design the invita-tion using a stamp of Santa carrying his sack of gifts to "deliver". A child's birthday party invitation could feature his or her favorite sport or hobby—baseball, soccer, music, horseback riding. With such a variety of wonderful designs available, feel free to use your imagination!

Color

Deciding what colors of ink, paper, embossing powder, and pens to use is sometimes determined by tradition—red and white for Valentine's Day, green and red for Christmas, pastels for Easter, black and orange for Halloween. Color is a very powerful factor in both art and craft because it will evoke particular feelings.

Color is a very powerful factor in both art and craft because it will evoke particular feelings.

Combinations of colors, too, can change the entire mood of a piece. For example, a wedding card might be done up in traditional white or ivory with a touch of light yellow for contrast. To reflect another style and change the feeling of the card, try using the palest gray with a contrast of burgundy.

An unconventional combination for the same wedding card might be navy blue, cream and lime green, which, if cleverly combined, could result in an attractive card, yet would elicit a different mood than the first two. Surprising things happen when you experiment with color! Here is some basic color theory information to help guide you on your color choices:

Referring to the Color Wheel, note that primary colors are yellow, red, and blue. Secondary colors green, orange, and purple are made by combining two primary colors. Tertiary colors are made by combining a primary color with an adjacent secondary color.

PRIMARY · TERTIARY · SECONDARY · TERTIARY · PRIMARY · TERTIARY · SECONDARY · TERTIARY · PRIMARY · SECONDARY · TERTIARY · PRIMARY

Color Wheel

Further study of the color wheel shows complementary colors, which are situated across from each other. Using complementary colors in stamping projects can create a great deal of contrast. Unless done intentionally, these colors in their purest form should be used conservatively, for the intensity of color would be competitive.

Analogous colors share a common primary or secondary color. For example, two to five colors adjacent to primary blue on the color wheel would be considered an analogous color palette. The effect is generally harmonious and pleasing.

Yellow, red, and blue form a triangle on the color wheel. These colors form a triadic palette. The effect is agreeable, and as with complementary colors, the intensity of the colors in their purest form creates a striking contrast.

Your choices will establish how warm, cool, or natural the colors in your project are.

Achromatic colors (not shown on the color wheel) are white, black, and various values of gray. Colors are tinted by adding white and shaded by introducing black. Papers, paints, and ink are available in a full range of tints and shades, offering endless color choices.

Begin by selecting complementary, analogous, or triadic colors from the color wheel. Introduce lighter or darker tints and shades to determine the mood or feeling of your project. Your choices will establish how warm, cool, or neutral the colors in your project are. Generally yellows, reds, and oranges are warm colors; blues, greens, and purples give a cool feeling; gray and beige tones are considered neutral.

Another agreeable color combination is a monochromatic color scheme. Monochromatic is a single color in a range of dark and light shades. To this color scheme, add interest by introducing a contrasting complimentary color.

Start with the color wheel as a guide and feel free to experiment—essentially it all boils down to what looks good.

Design

We've found that most stampers/crafters are visually oriented. That is, we need to see examples to feed the creative urge. Take a look around to inspire your stamping. Our environment is visually rich with designs, whether it be found in nature or in an art museum. Nature offers us the best in color combinations, patterns, and shapes. Our shops are full of merchandise—clothing, jewelry, dishware, sheets, towels, and rugs. Store displays and merchandise packaging provide a wealth of design ideas. Books and magazines are another endless resource. Even television and movies can give us quick glimpses at visuals to inspire us. Museums house works of art in which we may see aspects of color or perspective from another artist's viewpoint. So many things can provide that "Aha! This gives me an idea!" spark we all need to work our craft.

Collect books and magazines, take photographs and clip articles and pictures. Carry pen and paper to jot down notes when you see something that gives you a stamping idea. Refer back to those pictures and notes when you are ready to stamp.

Nature offers us the best in color combinations, patterns, and shapes.

Once you have determined a theme, selected colors, and have an inspiration to move forward with your stamping project, be prepared for your creation to go through changes as you're working along. Allow for deviations from your original design, for this fascinating process is a good part of what stamping is about. In fact, most samples in this book are a result of allowing materials to make shifts and turns from the original plan.

There exist, however, some basic rules of composition that you ought not lose sight of as your creative juices get flowing:

• **Focal point**—this is what your eyes will focus on first. It is what you would consider the main subject. It might feature a stamp, photograph, or a treasured finding. Sometimes the focus is a border, or an exotic handmade paper, or even an interesting fold in a card. Choose a primary focal point, then add a secondary focal point if you like, but beware of crowding a picture with too many subjects competing for attention. Additional elements should complement and support the main focal point. It's easy to make the mistake of adding too much—too many stamps, too much color or trim. Sometimes less is more!

Allow for deviations from your original design, for this fascinating process is a good part of what stamping is about.

• **Balance**—refers to the visual "weight" of parts in a picture. If arrangement of elements on a card feels terribly off–balance, your mind will try to compensate for it. You'll focus on the part of the picture that appears disproportionately lighter and attempt to see something there. Your eye is trying to compose a picture with a better distribution of weight to give a more integrated feeling.

Try to equalize visual weight in an off–balance piece by stamping several smaller or lighter color images in open area. Crop excess paper, change color of a piece of paper, ink, embossing powder or pen. A strategically placed bit of trim or ribbon might solve the problem.

Remember, though, that balance doesn't necessarily mean symmetrical. Not everything has to be perfectly centered or have equal margins. Open areas on a card are in proportion to the stamped sections and don't need to be filled in. By observing and studying well–designed images, you'll be training your eyes to sense balance in your compositions.

• **Finishing**—a stamped project that needs a finish is like a beautiful painting that needs to be matted or framed. The mat or frame showcases the work. Some stamped pieces will require more finishing than others. Look at the piece—does it appear completed to you? Or does it need something?

The easiest way to finish a stamped tag or card is to back it with a larger piece of paper in a complementary color. Determine if stamped portion needs to be cropped, or have a decorative edge applied before it is backed.

The piece can then be adhered to a folded notecard. The stamped image can be double– or triple–backed with several layers before final mounting. Check for balance with colors as well as with width of borders.

Choose a primary focal point, then add a secondary focal point if you like, but be aware of crowding a picture with too many subjects competing for attention.

Lastly, if additional texture is needed, tie or adhere ribbon, trinkets, or natural trim. In the same way, projects other than cards may need to be finished with ribbon, trim, or findings. Always keep in mind when putting finishing touches on a project that "less is more".

Everyday

Lilac Card

❧Stamp and emboss image on cardstock with embossing ink and powder. Color image, using brush pens.

❧Tear top and bottom edges of stamped cardstock. Fold colored paper in half to create card.

❧Stamp and emboss words on front bottom of card. Assemble and adhere card by layering papers as shown in photo.

Butterfly Photo Frame Card

❧Stamp and emboss image on photo frame card with embossing ink and powder. Color images, using brush pens. Adhere bow and picture to card front as shown in photo.

Special Thanks Card

❧Stamp and emboss words on colored paper with embossing ink and powder. Tear around image.

❧Stamp and emboss images on card. Emboss edges of stamped paper with glue pen and powder. Color images, using brush pens.

❧Adhere looped ribbon to card front. Assemble and adhere card by layering papers over ribbon as shown in photo.

34

Love Will Find a Way Card

1. Stamp and emboss image on center of vellum with embossing ink and powder.

2. Color image, using brush pen. Stamp images around first image with pigment ink. Let dry.

3. Cut square from center piece of cardstock and tear bottom edge. Stamp and emboss words on cardstock with embossing ink and powder.

4. Assemble card and adhere bow and charm to top left corner as shown in photo.

Heart Frame Friendship Card

⚭Stamp and emboss frame image on handmade card with embossing ink and powder. Tear around image. Water–emboss image, using technique for Water Embossing on pages 16–17.

⚭Color images, using brush pens and technique for Watercoloring on page 14. Place image over card and hold in place. Cut out center image, cutting through front flap of card. Place piece of wide, sheer ribbon between layers and adhere together.

⚭Stamp words inside card, visible through window, with dye–based ink. Adhere ribbon bow to card front.

Filigree Heart Invitation

1. Stamp and emboss image on enclosure card with embossing ink and powder. Stamp and emboss box around image with embossing ink and powder.

2. Water–emboss center image, using technique for Water Embossing on pages 16–17. Color image, using brush pens.

3. Stamp and emboss invitation image inside enclosure card. Adhere enclosure card to inside of handmade card, centering over fold. Score inside right and left flaps and fold so flaps meet in center. Cut half of heart shape from edge of each flap.

4. Emboss edge of heart with glue pen and powder. Punch two small holes and thread sheer ribbon through holes. Tie ribbon into bows.

5. Stamp words on bottom of flecked stamped paper with permanent ink. Let dry and lay on top of right side of photo frame.

6. Gently close frame. Stamp small image on thin strip of flecked paper with home decor ink. Wrap strip around closed frame and secure.

Heritage Roses Card

Stamp and emboss image on cardstock with embossing ink and powder. Color image, using brush pens and technique for Watercoloring on page 14.

Tear around image. Emboss word on front bottom of card. Cut pieces of colored paper. Assemble and adhere card by layering papers as shown in photo.

Acanthus Card

Stamp and emboss letter on card with embossing ink and powder. Color image, using brush pens. Mask letter, using technique for Masking on page 18. Stamp image four times with dye–based ink.

Unfold card and cut image into square, using craft knife and straight edge. Adhere stamped square to inside of card.

Emboss edges of square window on front of card with embossing pen and powder.

Double Frame Gift

1. Stamp large images on one side of large piece of handmade paper with home decor ink. Let dry.

2. Cut two 4" x 5¾" pieces of thin cardboard. Place cutouts at top of unstamped side of paper, ½" apart. Wrap paper over edges and secure. Adhere strip of flecked paper over center gap.

3. Stamp images on two photo frame cards with home decor ink. Let dry.

4. Adhere to top of wrapped cardboard pieces, leaving a ⅜" gap. Place photographs within frames and adhere edges shut. Stamp image at top center of 4" x 5¾" flecked paper with home decor ink.

Congratulations Vellum Card

1. Stamp images on card with multipurpose ink; heat–set.

2. Color images, using brush pen. Fold piece of vellum over card and adhere to back of card.

3. Unfold small envelope and trace onto piece of vellum. Assemble vellum envelope. Stamp and emboss back of vellum envelope with tinted embossing ink and powder.

4. Stuff envelope with red hearts and adhere to card as shown in photo. Adhere bow to card.

Rose Pop–up Card

1. Stamp image on cardstock, using small pigment ink pads to separately color teapot and roses. Emboss image with powder. Color image, using brush pens; cut out.

2. Cut 8" x 4½" rectangle from cardstock. Crease rectangle in half horizontally to create notecard.

3. Stamp and emboss isolated roses on inside top of notecard with pigment ink and embossing powder. Stamp bunches of roses, which will become layers

of pop–up card. Be certain flower bunches are arranged to coordinate with layers that will go in front and back.

4. Stamp three separate rose bunches on cardstock; small, medium, and large. Color and cut out all layers, leaving long "tail" in middle of each. Emboss word on colored paper with embossing ink and powder.

5. Tear a square of mulberry paper and a smaller square of colored paper. Adhere papers to bottom of card.

6. Trace Pop–up Mechanism Pattern on page 37 onto cardstock; cut out. Fold and adhere to card. Ensure card opens and closes correctly.

7. Adhere teapot to front of pop–up mechanism with double–sided foam tape. Slip rose bunch layers through slots in pop–up mechanism and make adjustments in length of tails, if necessary.

8. Score horizontal line ¼" up from bottom of each tail. Adhere tails below scored line to bottom of card, continuing to ensure card will open and shut correctly.

Adding flowers to Rose Pop-up card.

Half completed Rose Pop-up card.

Pop–up Mechanism Pattern

Mountain Fold

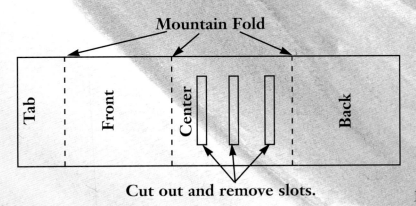

Tab | Front | Center | Back

Cut out and remove slots.

Pattern is actual size

I Miss You Fish Card

❧Score card along fold. Stamp images on card with dye–based inks. Cut two pieces of tracing paper the same size as card.

❧Stamp and emboss words on tracing paper with embossing ink and powder. Place over cards and punch three small holes through left side of papers. Thread colored raffia through holes and tie knots.

Starfish Card

❧Water–emboss images on cardstock, using technique for Water Embossing on pages 16–17. Let dry.

❧Color images, using brush pens and technique for Watercoloring on page 14.

❧Tear piece of handmade paper and emboss edges with glue pen and tapestry powder. Tear piece of mulberry paper. Assemble and adhere card by layering papers on front of card as shown in photo.

Lighthouse Card

1. Stamp image on a small glass square with home decor ink, using technique for Stamping on Glass, Ceramics & Porcelain on pages 20–21. Paint stamped glass with porcelain paints. Let dry.

2. Mask image, using technique for Masking on page 18. Sponge paint to create sky, using technique for Sponging on page 26. Let dry. Sponge below image with home decor ink to create beach. Let dry.

3. Stamp and emboss word on cardstock. Tear around image and adhere to bottom front of handmade card.

4. Punch holes through front of card. Thread tassel through hole in stamped glass, then through holes in card. Adhere end of tassel to card.

Florentine Letters Tri–fold Card

🍃Stamp letters on cardstock with pigment ink. Let dry; cut out. Score paper in thirds, so front left flap is ¾" shorter than full width of card.

🍃Emboss edge of front left flap with glue pen and embossing powder. Attach piece of ribbon onto front and back of card with tape. Tie ribbon knot on right side of card.

🍃Assemble and adhere cutout letters to paper and cut in rectangle.

I Miss You Magnolia Card

🍃Stamp image on cardstock with multipurpose ink. Color image, using brush pens.

🍃Cut image into a square. Tear and cut graduating–sized squares of colored paper, larger than stamped square. Stamp words on bottom front of handmade card with pigment ink. Let dry.

🍃Assemble and adhere card by layering papers as shown in photo. Punch holes in left front side of card. Trim card with charm and ribbon bow.

Sandpaper Petroglyphs Card

꘍Stamp images on piece of torn sandpaper with multipurpose ink. Stamp additional image on separate piece of sandpaper and cut out. Color image, using brush pen as shown in photo.

꘍Sponge along edges of stamped sandpaper with embossing ink and cosmetic sponge; emboss with powders. Adhere to folded corrugated paper. Attach cut–out image on card with double–sided foam tape.

꘍Punch two holes on each side of card. Thread black leather strips through holes and tie.

Zuni Indian Pot Card

꘍Stamp image on cardstock with multipurpose ink. Color image, using brush pens and technique for Watercoloring on page 14.

꘍Adhere to inside of oval photo frame card. Stamp images on front of frame card, using brush pen and technique for Coloring & Painting on the Stamp on page 14.

Navajo Serape Card

꘍Stamp and emboss image on cardstock with pigment ink and powder. Tear side edges of stamped cardstock. Color image, using brush pens, and adhere to card.

Brushed Rose Thank You Card

❧Water–emboss image, using technique for Water Embossing on pages 16–17. Stamp and emboss image and word on card with embossing ink and powder.

❧Tear right side edges of card. Wrap cord around fold and tie into bow. Highlight rose with home decor ink.

Sympathy Card

❧Stamp and emboss word on handmade card with embossing ink and powder. Emboss edge of card with glue pen and powder. Stamp and emboss image on torn piece of handmade cardstock.

❧Color image, using brush pens, and emboss one edge with glue pen and powder. Stamp images on handmade paper with home decor ink and tear around image. Assemble and adhere card by layering papers as shown in photo.

Accordion–fold Anniversary Card

1. Stamp botanical images on cardstock with multi-purpose ink. Color images, using brush pens and technique for Watercoloring on page 14. Cut images in identical squares. Make one image much smaller.

2. Assemble cards to form an accordion of five panels. Randomly stamp words on front of card with metallic ink. Repeat random stamping of words at top and bottom of remaining panels with metallic ink. Edge second and fourth stamped panels with metallic ink.

3. Adhere images to assorted colors of mulberry paper. Adhere smaller square to mulberry and graduated sizes of handmade paper.

4. Adhere looped ribbon to bottom front of card. Adhere layered pieces to panels as shown in photo.

Letter B Card

☙ Stamp image on cardstock square with multi-purpose ink. Color image, using brush pens. Brush around edges of stamped square with home decor ink, using sponge brush.

☙ Assemble and adhere paper layers and cord on front of card as shown in photo.

Valentine's Day

Heart of Hearts Card

See photo on page 46.

1. Stamp image on vellum paper with pigment ink. Cut image from paper, leaving ¼" border.

2. Trace over stamped image, using burnishing tool on wrong side of paper, to create raised effect on right side of paper. Do not push too hard or tool may pierce paper.

3. Color desired portions of image on wrong side of paper, using brush pen. Make template of stamped image and trace onto front of card.

4. Cut out image to create window on front of card. Mount stamped vellum behind window. Mount colored paper behind vellum.

5. Adhere ribbon bow to front of card.

Three Hearts Card

See photo on page 46.

- Stamp and emboss handmade card with embossing ink and powder. Cut out center image to create window.

- Draw small red heart on inside of card visible through window, using pen. Adhere tiny bows to front of card.

LOVE Card

See photo on page 46.

- Stamp letters on cardstock with home decor ink.

- Cut out stamped images and attach to vellum with double–sided tape as shown in photo. Adhere vellum and ribbon bow to front of card.

43

Heart–shaped Chipwood Boxes

- Paint a set of three heart-shaped chipwood boxes with acrylic paints. Stamp images on boxes with home decor ink. Lightly brush ink over edges of boxes, using sponge brush.

Be Mine Valentine Card

❧Cut window on right side of card. Stamp and emboss words on left side of window with embossing ink and powder.

❧Stamp image on cardstock with dye–based ink and cut out. Attach to inside of card, visible through window. Attach bow and charm onto front of card.

Clematis & Jasmine Heart

❧Stamp and emboss image on cardstock with embossing ink and powder. Color image, using brush pens and technique for Watercoloring on page 14.

❧Cut top and bottom edges of stamped paper, using decorative scissors. Lightly sponge around edges of card with home decor ink or acrylic paint, using technique for Sponging on page 26.

❧Assemble and adhere card by layering papers as shown in photo. Tie ribbon around fold.

Filigree Heart Beaded Card

❧Stamp and emboss image on cardstock with embossing ink and powder. Cut stamped paper into rectangle. Color image, using brush pens and technique for Watercoloring on page 14.

❧String three short strands of beads. Poke strands through stamped paper, knotting ends on back side to secure.

❧Randomly stamp images on card with metallic ink. Tear handmade papers into random shapes. Assemble and adhere card by layering papers as shown in photo.

Roses Heart Frame Card

1. Make a reversed mold, using stamp and technique for Working with Modeling Compounds on pages 22–23.

2. While paper modeling compound is wet, cut out center of image to create frame and separate heart pin. Smooth rough edges of pin with fingers. Let pieces dry.

3. Paint raised parts and inside edge of frame with home decor ink. Stamp image on pin.

4. Lightly dab around edge of pin with home decor ink, using sponge brush. Adhere pin backing to back of pin.

5. Cut and fold stationery paper to fit inside card. Stamp words on right side of stationery.

6. Ink portions of large frame stamp to isolate rose images. Color rose images on card and paper modeling compound, using brush pens and technique for Watercoloring on page 14.

7. Cut two diagonal slits into left side of stationery to hold photograph. Insert stamped stationery into notecard and tie cord around folded edge to secure.

8. Tear piece of handmade paper to fit front of card. Assemble and adhere card by layering with handmade paper and frame as shown in photo.

9. Place pin in center of frame and pin to card.

Double Heart Card

☙ Make reverse mold with stamp, using techniques for Working with Modeling Compounds on pages 22–23. Press paper modeling compound into mold.

☙ Cut out individual images and smooth edges with finger. Let dry and paint with acrylic paints. Adhere tissue paper and paper modeling compound images to front of card.

Love Buttons Card

☙ Roll paper modeling compound into six small balls and flatten balls into button–size circles. Smooth rough edges with fingers and poke two holes side by side in centers of buttons. Heat–dry.

☙ Stamp images on buttons and around edges of card with multipurpose ink. Sew buttons onto front of card with twine.

Heart Full of Hearts Card

❧Cut piece of handmade paper to fit card. Cut heart shape from white paper to create stencil. Center stencil over handmade paper and stamp, overlapping images with multipurpose ink. Stamp one image with home decor ink and fill in, using a paintbrush. Cut slits in handmade paper and slide piece of ribbon through slits as shown in photo. Adhere stamped paper to front of card.

Round Rose Box

1. Stamp images on ribbon with home decor ink. Color images, using brush pens.

2. Adhere colored mulberry paper to cover box lid and bottom, tacking edges inside. Tie stamped ribbon into bow and adhere to box lid.

3. Stamp image on cardstock with home decor ink. Color image, using brush pens.

4. Tear around image. Adhere metallic tissue to folded cardstock to create tag.

5. Tear small piece of mulberry paper. Adhere layers of paper to outside of tag as shown in photo. Attach tag to box.

Tulip Stencil Birthday Card

1. Stamp and emboss on iridescent flecked paper with embossing ink and pearl powder. Color image, using brush pens.

2. Wrap piece of thin cardboard with stamped paper. Tie ribbon around wrapped cardboard and knot. Adhere wrapped cardboard to front of contrasting colored card.

3. Stamp and emboss image on precut tag with embossing ink and pearl powder.

4. Adhere tag to torn piece of handmade paper and punch hole in corner of tag. Thread ribbon through hole and around ribbon knot, securing with a bow.

Rose Gift Bag

1. Stamp images on paper with home decor ink. Color images, using brush pens and technique for Watercoloring on page 14.

2. Fold stamped paper into bag, using technique for Making a Bag on page 27. Fold top of bag and punch two holes near top of bag.

3. Stamp images on front of folded cardstock, using technique for Masking on page 18. Cut around image, but not through tips of leaves at fold.

4. Thread ribbon through holes and attach tag as shown in photo.

Fun Birthday Card

1. Stamp and emboss image on flecked cardstock with embossing ink and powder. Cut small horizontal slit in center of card just above stamped image, using craft knife.

2. Stamp images on assorted colors of torn handmade paper with complementary colors of pigment ink. Let dry.

3. Arrange papers in bunch, adding bullion pieces to bunch. Place bunch in slot and adhere to back of card.

4. Cut metallic cardstock slightly larger than stamped card. Assemble and adhere card by layering papers as shown in photo.

Beaded Cake Card

1. Stamp and emboss image on cardstock with embossing ink and powder. Color image, using brush pens.

2. Cut around image to create circle, using deckle–edged scissors. Sew beads onto card at top of image.

3. Cut circle out of top center of card for window. Adhere circle to inside of card, visible through window.

4. Apply sparkle glue around front edge of window. Adhere cord bow to front of card below window.

Party Hat

1. Stamp assorted images on two different colored tissue papers with metallic ink. Let dry.

2. Trace Party Hat Pattern onto white cardstock and cut out. Adhere stamped tissue papers to hat with spray adhesive. Trim excess tissue from hat.

3. Tape bunch of mylar strips together on one end and adhere taped end to inside top of hat with strips protruding from top.

4. Fold hat and adhere, with images and mylar strips on outside of hat. Punch small holes on sides of hat.

5. Thread satin ribbon through holes and tie bows as shown in photo.

49

Party Hat Pattern

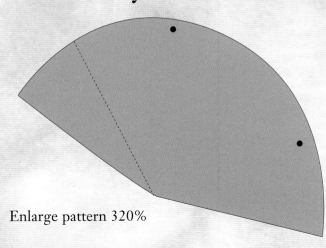

Enlarge pattern 320%

Bear Gift Wrap

1. Stamp images on scrap paper. Cut out each and determine placement on top of wrapping paper.

2. Lightly draw squares and rectangles around images to fit together, using pencil. Square up boxes, using pencil and straight edge.

3. Stamp images on wrapping paper with assorted pigment inks. Let dry, then wrap gift.

4. Fold cardstock and stamp top of image near fold to create gift tag. Cut around top of image, avoiding fold. Punch hole near top of tag.

5. Wrap ribbon around gift and tie into bow, attaching gift tag to ribbon.

Morning Glory Journal

This project demonstrates the effect achieved by curling and shaping paper cutouts. Place cutouts on a soft surface, such as a felt pad and then rub with a burnisher or stylus to curve paper. Adhere pieces to maintain the three–dimensional effect place tiny pieces of foam tape or drops of quick–drying silicone under raised and curved papers. The best papers to use are heavier to maintain shaping. Lightweight papers may be used if first adhered to cardstock before shaping.

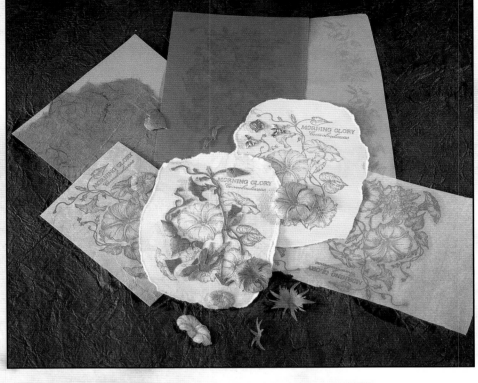

1. Stamp image on art paper with pigment ink, creating original image. Tear around stamped image.

2. Stamp image on art paper with pigment ink, cutting out trumpet–shaped flower bodies and starburst–shaped flower centers. Curl centers, shaping only largest pieces. Adhere trumpet shapes to original image.

3. Stamp image on handmade paper with pigment ink. Cut out buds and adhere in place on original image. Cut out flower heads and cut petals apart, leaving them attached at center of flower. Curl petals.

4. Stamp image on art paper with pigment ink. Cut out leaves and stems. Curl leaves. Adhere stems flat to image, then use drop of silicone or piece of foam tape under leaves.

5. Adhere flower heads to original image only at centers where petals join. Place drop of silicone or double–sided foam tape under each petal.

6. Adhere starburst shapes over center of flower heads only at centers.

7. Create left margin of cover by using brayer and technique for Brayering on page 25. Roll brayer across pigment inks to deposit blended rainbow of color onto paper. Roll brayer on tissue three times, creating a strip of fade–out rainbow hues. Stamp small images on strip with same three colors, which appear bolder than brayered color.

8. Stamp two pieces of tissue paper with image and adhere to right of three–dimensional image. Carefully tear tissue to retain only parts of image wanted, and adhere upside down.

9. Assemble assorted, stamped, and torn papers to create cover of journal, maintaining three–dimensional collage as focal point.

10. Attach charms to complete cover.

Four Women Scarf

1. Stamp images on hand-dyed, scarf-shaped fabric 1½" from bottom edge with home decor ink, using technique for Stamping on Fabric on page 19. Let dry.

2. Stretch fabric over frame. Apply gutta resist around images in stripes and zigzags to form painting areas. Paint with desired colors. Let dry.

3. Remove fabric from frame and heat–set. Wash out resist.

4. Paint accent color along edges with home decor ink. Hem scarf edges. Paint used necessitates careful handwashing of scarf.

Four Women Birthday Card

1. Cut piece of fabric large enough to stretch over frame or box. Lay fabric flat on work surface. Stamp image with home decor ink. Dry image, using heat tool.

2. Stretch and secure fabric smoothly over frame or box, using push pins.

3. Brush enough water only onto image area to thoroughly moisten fabric. Stroke paint on fabric, allowing colors to blend slightly. Dry, using heat tool.

4. Remove fabric from frame. Cut piece of batting slightly smaller than stamped image.

5. Brush colored stripe along inside bottom edge of cardstock with textile paints.

6. Cut away ragged edge from bottom front edge of cardstock. Painted edge should show below ragged edge when card is closed.

7. Adhere batting and stamped fabric to front center of card. The simplest method of adhering is using adhesive spray on reverse side of fabric/batting and pressing to cardstock. Smooth down fabric edges. Trim top and bottom of fabric if necessary.

8. Cut piece of handmade paper ¼" larger than folded cardstock. Cut rectangle from center, same size and shape as stamped image. Adhere handmade paper onto front of card to frame image. Trim excess paper from outside edges of cardstock, wrapping excess at top over fold onto back of card.

9. Tear off handmade paper at bottom along ragged edge previously cut. Paint a line along torn edge with home decor ink, using a watercolor paintbrush.

Four Women Scarf Gift Box

1. Stamp images on ribbon with home decor ink. Let dry.

2. Cut mulberry paper to fit box lid. Stamp images on cut mulberry paper with home decor ink. Wrap box lid with stamped paper, adhering into place with spray adhesive or glue stick.

3. Cut strip of mulberry paper wide enough to wrap all four sides of box, overlapping on edges. Stamp images on strip with home decor ink, lining up images with those on lid and continuing around sides of box.

4. Wrap sides with stamped strip and adhere in place. Cut mulberry paper to fit inside of box and adhere in place.

5. Tie ribbon into bow and adhere to box lid.

54

Bow Card

1. Stamp and emboss image on cardstock with embossing ink and powder.

2. Emboss image, using technique for Water–embossing on pages 16–17.

3. Cut slits in cardstock where ribbon will thread through, using craft knife, as shown in photo.

4. Thread one piece of ribbon through slits vertically and one piece horizontally.

5. Adhere ribbon ends to back of cardstock. Adhere cardstock to front of card.

6. Wrap cord around fold of card and tie into bow.

Water–embossed Birthday Card

❧Stamp and emboss words on card with embossing ink and powder. Stamp image, using technique for Coloring & Painting on the Stamp on page 14.

❧Emboss image on card, using technique for Water–embossing on pages 16–17.

❧Thread beads onto bullion and tie around card fold.

Quaking Aspen Leaf Card

❧Stamp overlapping images, light to dark, on cardstock with multipurpose ink. Heat–set and cut around image to form a square.

❧Adhere image to front of card and add accents, using brush pen. Stamp image below square with multipurpose ink as shown in photo.

Pixie Birthday Invitation

❧Stamp row of images on envelope flap with alternating colors of dye–based ink. Stamp same images and write message on card with dye–based ink and pen.

❧Cut around edges of card, using arabesque–edge scissors. Cut colored cardstock slightly larger than message card and adhere as shown in photo.

Easter

Botanical Stationery Set

1. Stamp images on eggshell paper with dye–based ink.

2. Spray adhesive on back of paper, then wrap lid and box with paper.

3. Cut pieces of paper to fit inside lid and inside box as liners. Spray liners with adhesive. Adhere liner to lid.

4. Lay wide ribbon inside box and adhere liner to top of ribbon.

5. Stamp images on cards and envelopes with dye–based ink.

6. Bundle stationery together with twine and attach charm. Place lid on box and tie ribbon into bow.

Windmill Crackle Box

1. Prepare prepurchased wood box with crackle finish according to manufacturer's instructions.

2. Stamp images onto notecards with dye–based ink. Cut out one image and glue to top of lid.

3. Cut satin ribbon into two pieces. Tape end of one ribbon to inside center of box. Adhere one end of second ribbon to inside center of lid.

4. Cut pieces of handmade paper for inside box and lid. Adhere paper to lid and box with spray adhesive. Ribbon may be used to close box by tying bow.

Primula Botanical Card

🐾Stamp and emboss image on cardstock with embossing ink and powder. Color image, using brush pens and technique for Watercoloring on page 14.

🐾Tear top and bottom edges of cardstock and emboss edges with glue pen. Adhere cardstock to handmade card.

Floral Stationery Box & Card Set

🐾Stamp and emboss images onto large piece of paper with embossing ink and powder. Color images, using brush pens. Stamp additional images over previous images with dye–based ink as shown in photo.

🐾Spray adhesive on back of paper, then wrap lid and box with paper. Stamp images on envelopes, and stamp and emboss images on cards. Color images on cards, using brush pens.

🐾Tie ribbon around stationery and place in box.

Easter Egg Invitation

🐾Stamp and emboss image on cardstock with embossing ink and powder. Cut image into rectangle and emboss edges with embossing pen.

🐾Stamp and emboss images on card. Color images, using brush pens and technique for Watercoloring on page 14.

🐾Tear piece of handmade paper. Assemble and adhere card by layering papers as shown in photo. Adhere bow to side of card.

Sunflower Birdhouse

1. Trace Birdhouse Patterns on page 59 onto grass and straw cardstock.

2. Stamp and emboss house with pigment ink and powder. Color images, using brush pens.

3. Assemble house, following Birdhouse Assembly Instructions on page 58. Tie raffia into small bundles and adhere to roof for thatched appearance. Assemble chimney. Adhere chimney to roof.

4. Attach roof supports and adhere roof to house.

Feather Medley Birdhouse

1. Trace Birdhouse Patterns on page 59 onto tan flecked cardstock for house and bark–like handmade paper for roof.

2. Stamp images on house with multipurpose ink. Color images, using brush pens and technique for Watercoloring on page 14.

3. Assemble house, following Birdhouse Assembly Instructions on page 58. Attach roof supports, and adhere roof to house.

4. Adhere twigs along roof, around heart–shaped hole, and underneath hole for perch.

Rosebud Birdhouse

1. Trace Birdhouse Patterns on page 59 onto flecked cardstock.

2. Stamp and emboss images on house with embossing ink and alternating colors of powder. Stamp another image on house with metallic ink. Color images, using brush pens.

3. Assemble house, following Birdhouse Assembly Instructions on page 58. Trim house with ribbon and cording. Adhere dried moss and rosebuds to roof.

4. Wrap roof with bullion in crisscross pattern. Attach roof supports and adhere roof to house.

Wedding Chapel Birdhouse

1. Trace Birdhouse Patterns on page 59 onto white cardstock.

2. Stamp image on house, using technique for Coloring & Painting on the Stamp on page 14.

3. Assemble house, following Birdhouse Assembly Instructions on page 58. Trim house with lace, cording, and trinket. Adhere paper doily to roof. Adhere lace at edges of roof.

4. Attach roof supports and adhere roof to house. Assemble cupola. Thread cording through top of brass bell and adhere to inside top of cupola. Adhere cupola to roof.

Birdhouse Assembly Instructions

1. Lightly trace all lines from Birdhouse Pattern on page 59 onto back of paper, using a sharp pencil. Fold lines are dashed and cut lines are solid.

2. Cut out shapes, using scissors or craft knife and straight edge. Lightly score and erase all dashed lines to make paper easier to fold.

3. Decorate birdhouse as instructed on page 57.

58 4. Assemble house: apply glue to bottom and side tabs and press them to inside.

5. Assemble roof: apply glue to unnotched side of roof support. With notched side facing outward, align folded edge of roof support with drawn guideline on underside of roof. See Diagram A. Repeat for other roof support. Let dry.

6. Bend roof so that angle matches top of birdhouse. Apply drop of glue on roof support tabs near notch. Press two sides together and let dry. Thus secures roof at proper angle. See Diagram B. If desired, apply glue to outside of roof supports and press to permanently attach roof to birdhouse.

7. Add shingles: cut all 10 pieces where indicated. Starting with shingle piece #2, apply glue to top half of underside and align with bottom edge of roof. See Diagram C. Repeat with shingle piece #3. See Diagram D. Continue gluing, alternating shingle pieces #2 and #3, until each side of roof has 4 shingle pieces. Glue shingle piece #1 to each side of roof so that they meet at center of roof. See Diagram E.

8. Assemble cupola: apply glue to side tab and press to inside, forming a cube with tabs at top and bottom. Apply glue to 4 top tabs and pinch triangular flaps together, forming a point. Attach to roof by applying glue to bottom tabs, folding up inside, and pressing to roof.

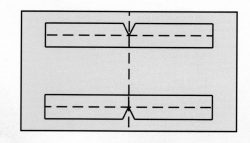

Diagram A

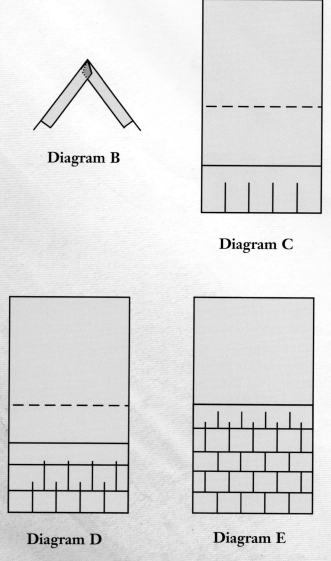

Diagram B

Diagram C

Diagram D

Diagram E

Birdhouse Patterns

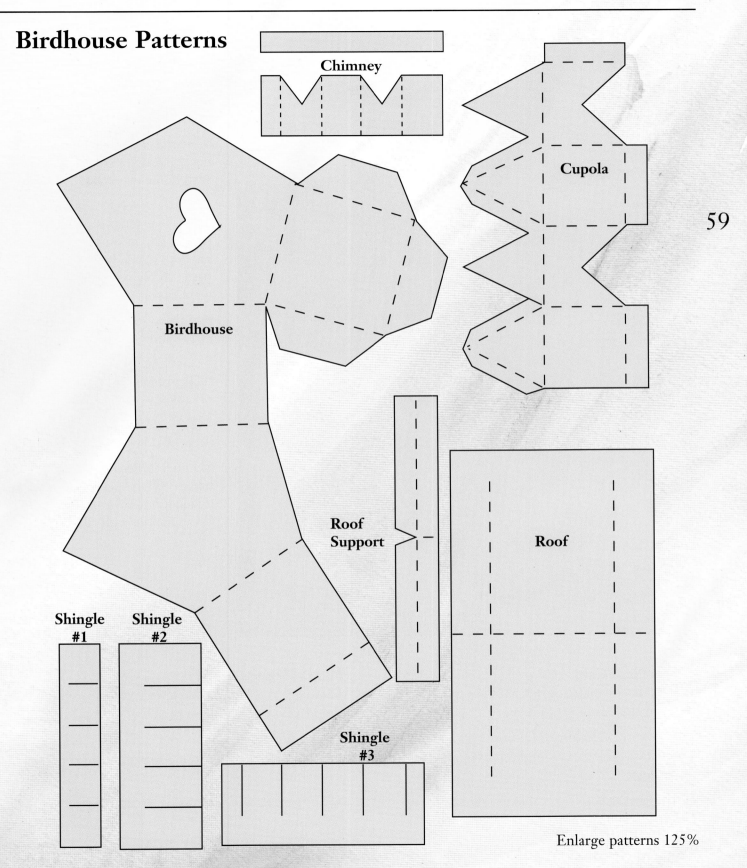

Chimney

Cupola

Birdhouse

Roof
Support

Roof

Shingle
#1

Shingle
#2

Shingle
#3

Enlarge patterns 125%

60

Easter Basket

1. Blow eggs. Stamp eggs with multipurpose ink.

2. Stamp paper for outside of basket with multipurpose ink.

3. Stamp and emboss hand-made paper for inside of basket with home decor ink.

4. Cover mold with plastic wrap. Tear scrap paper into pieces. Dip in water to dampen, then dip in papier maché paste. Apply papers to mold to form basket. Let dry.

5. Adhere stamped papers to inside and outside of basket with spray adhesive.

6. Tear paper around top edges of basket.

7. Paint edges with home decor ink.

8. Punch holes in side of basket. Attach piece of wire through holes for handle. Wrap handle with ribbon.

Chicks Place Card

☙ Stamp image on cardstock with multipurpose ink. Color image, using brush pens.

☙ Score horizontal line to fold card, avoiding stamped images. Cut around top of image above scored line.

☙ Trim card so top flap is shorter than back flap. Adhere handmade paper to inside of card.

Bunnies Place Card

☙ Stamp image on cardstock with permanent ink. Color image, using brush pens.

☙ Score horizontal line to fold card, avoiding stamped images. Cut around top of image above scored line.

☙ Cut front flap of card, using decorative scissors. Color strip along inside bottom of card, using brush pen. Emboss edges of card with embossing pen and powder.

Bunny Tea Card

☙Stamp and emboss image on cardstock with pigment ink and embossing powder. Color image, using brush pens.

☙Stamp multiple images on card with pigment ink. Stamp and emboss image on bottom of card with pigment ink and embossing powder.

☙Tear top and bottom edges of corrugated paper and assemble and adhere card by layering papers as shown in photo.

Origami Egg Pocket Package

☙Cut two different pieces of handmade paper into 6" x 9" rectangles. Stamp scattered pattern on one piece of paper with alternating colors of multi-purpose ink.

☙Spray light coat of adhesive onto wrong side of papers and adhere together. To make pocket, follow Origami Egg Pocket Package Diagrams on page 62. Tie ribbon around completed pocket.

Origami Egg Pocket Package Diagrams

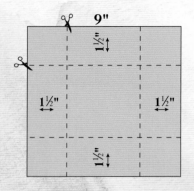

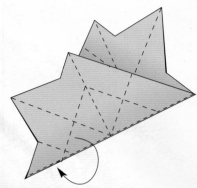

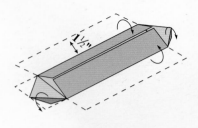

1 Lay paper on work surface, stamped side up. Measure and cut 1½" squares from each corner.

2 Valley–fold top and bottom edges to middle so edges meet in center. Crease well.

3 Mountain–fold short side flaps to back.

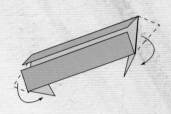

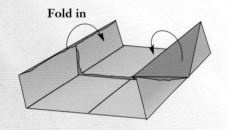

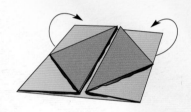

4 Valley–fold sides to center and crease. Paper should now be 3" x 3" square.

5 Open paper. Lay stamped side face down. Diaper–fold and adhere each corner of short side flaps to form an "arrow" point.

6 Diaper–fold bottom right corner to top left corner, but only crease from edge of inner creased square to outer point. Keep center "square" crease–free.

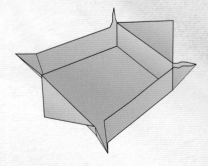

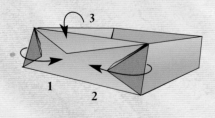

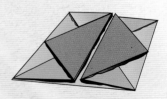

7 Open. Repeat diaper fold on opposite angle. Crease outward to both points. Remember to keep center crease–free.

8 Pinch point. Tuck under rectangular flaps on each side. Repeat with three other points. Adhere points down.

9 Push in and "collapse" top and bottom sides, using index fingers. Press pocket flat. Crease well.

Morning Glory Photo Frame

1. Paint frame with two coats of paint. Paint light-weight paper with thin coat of same paint.

2. Apply paint to stamp, using sponge brush and technique for Coloring & Painting on the Stamp on page 14. Stamp several times on painted paper, re-inking after each impression.

3. Thin paint with water for lighter, more trans-lucent shade of paint. Color stamped images with thinned paint, using fine–tip paintbrush.

4. Cut around outermost edges of painted images. Adhere cut out images to painted frame with spray adhesive, wrapping images around edges of frame.

5. Apply two–part china crackle glaze, following manufacturer's instructions. Emphasize cracks by lightly rubbing medium shade of paint over frame. Avoid rubbing too much paint over stamped images. Wipe off excess paint with soft cloth.

64

Morning Glory Card & Envelope

✍Stamp and emboss image on cardstock with embossing ink and powder. Repeat process on envelope flap.

✍Color images, using brush pens. Emboss inside edge of oval photo frame card with embossing pen and powder.

✍Mount cardstock to inside of photo frame card so image shows through window. Tie ribbon bow around fold of card.

Velvet Rose Card

✍Stamp images on velvet, using technique for Stamping on Velvet on page 20. Stamp images on photo frame card with metallic ink.

✍Attach velvet to inside front of card with double–sided tape. Open card and place a small piece of fiber batting on velvet.

✍Cut cardstock to fit over velvet and batting and adhere to card with spray adhesive. Glue cording around edge of front oval. Tie cording into bow around fold of card.

Cosmos Photo Frame Card

1. Stamp and emboss image on left side and lower right corner of card with embossing ink and powder. Stamp and emboss an additional image on scrap of same type of paper as card.

2. Color images, using brush pens.

3. Cut window in center right side of card. Cut motifs out of extra embossed image.

4. Attach cut–out images to card with double–sided tape as shown in photo. Draw a thin border around window, using ruler and brush pen.

5. Mount photo to inside of card and adhere edges together.

Grandmother's Card

Stamp and emboss around oval edge of frame card with embossing ink and powder. Color images, using brush pens.

Cut vellum into 7¾" x 5" piece. Fold in half. Stamp and emboss image on outside of folded vellum with embossing ink. Highlight top portion of image, using brush pen as shown in photo.

Run thin strip of craft glue near fold on underside of card and mount vellum to inside of card. Adhere bow to top corner of card.

Queen Anne's Lace Card

Stamp image on cardstock with dye–based ink. Color image, using brush pens. Assemble and adhere card by layering papers as shown in photo.

Watering Can Pin Card

1. Roll out clay modeling compound to ⅛" thickness, using technique for Working with Modeling Compounds on pages 22–23. Stamp image into clay for pin. Cut out image and smooth edges with fingers. Poke three holes in bottom of pin and bake.

66

2. Paint pin with acrylic paints, then coat with sealer. Put drop of craft glue on one end of three strands of cording and insert into pin holes. Thread charms onto cording and knot securely.

3. Adhere piece of torn handmade paper to inside of card. Adhere torn paper to front of card. Stamp images on front of card with metallic ink. Let dry.

4. Color images, using brush pens. Cut window in front of card for pin to fit through. Adhere pin backing to back of pin. Attach pin to inner part of card to appear through window as shown in photo.

Rose Earrings

☙Roll out clay modeling compound to ⅛" thickness, using technique for Working with Modeling Compounds on pages 22–23. Stamp image twice into clay for earrings. Cut around edges of images and remove excess clay. Smooth edges with fingers and bake.

☙Paint earrings with acrylic paints; coat with sealer. Adhere earring posts to back of earrings with jeweler's glue.

Wonderful Aunt Pin Card

1. Stamp image on cardstock with dye–based ink and tear out image. Color image, using brush pens. Stamp words on top left front of card with dye–based ink.

2. Roll out clay modeling compound to ¼" thickness, using technique for Working with Modeling Compounds on pages 22–23. Stamp image into clay and cut out for pin. Smooth edges with fingers and bake.

3. Paint pin with acrylic paints, then coat with sealer. Adhere pin backing to back of pin.

4. Assemble and adhere card by layering handmade papers as shown in photo. Attach pin to front of card.

Miniature Rose Chest

1. Remove drawer pulls from prepurchased, miniature wood chest. Paint chest and drawers with acrylic paint. Let dry. Sand several edges to create aged appearance. Wipe off dust.

2. Stamp images on paper with multipurpose ink and heat–set. Color images, using brush pens. Spray with fixative to avoid smearing.

3. Brush thin layer of découpage medium over sprayed images, using sponge brush. Let dry, then cut out images.

4. Brush thin layer of découpage medium to backs of images. Adhere images to top of chest and front of drawers, making certain all edges of images are secured.

5. Brush thin layer of découpage medium over images. Paint four beads with home decor ink. Let dry.

6. Cut slits between drawers, using very sharp craft knife, so drawers open. Brush découpage medium over any loose edges to secure.

7. Stamp image in all four corners on both sides of chest with home decor ink. Apply antique stain to chest, using soft cloth. Wipe off excess stain.

8. Attach drawer pulls to center of each drawer with instant adhesive. Glue painted beads to bottom of chest for feet.

Rose Accessory Box

Stamp partial image on 2" porcelain square with home decor ink. Paint image with porcelain paints, using fine–tip paintbrush. Bake according to manufacturer's instructions.

Adhere porcelain square to top of small brass jewelry box with jeweler's glue. Adhere cording around edge of square.

Letter Opener

Stamp partial image onto ¾" porcelain oval with multipurpose ink. Paint image with porcelain paints, using fine–tip paintbrush. Bake according to manufacturer's instructions.

Adhere oval into jewelry cameo holder with jeweler's glue. Glue holder onto end of prepurchased brass letter opener.

Brass Bookmark Clip

Stamp partial image on ½" porcelain circle with multipurpose ink. Paint image with porcelain paints, using fine–tip paintbrush. Bake according to manufacturer's instructions.

Adhere circle to end of prepurchased brass book mark clip with jeweler's glue. Glue cording around edge of circle.

Father's Day

Materials used to stamp the Winter Tree Tie.

Winter Tree Tie

1. Purchase solid–colored tie. Cut a tie from scratch paper, using Tie Pattern.

2. Design placement for stamped images on paper tie, remembering unstamped space is just as important as stamped areas.

3. Apply textile paint to stamp, using sponge brush. Stamp images on purchased tie, following placement on paper tie. Let dry.

4. Overstamp some images in different color textile paint. Stamp on top of, but not exactly over, selected images, leaving shadow of color showing as shown in photo. Let dry.

5. Stamp additional images on tie. Highlight edges or veins of additional images with contrasting textile paint. Let dry.

6. Heat–set images.

Tie Pattern

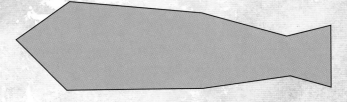

Enlarge pattern 500%

Marsh Wren Clock

ᶒ Stamp image on 3½" porcelain tile with home decor ink. Paint image with porcelain paints. Stain clock, following manufacturer's instructions. Insert clock face and clock works. Adhere tile to clock frame with silicone adhesive. Stain ⅛" molding. Cut molding into pieces to fit around tile for frame and adhere in place.

Tie Card

1. Stamp image in random pattern on piece of muslin with dye–based ink. Enlarge Tie Pattern on page 68 175%. Trace pattern onto stamped muslin and onto cardstock.

2. Cut out fabric and cardstock tie pieces. Stamp image on muslin tie with fabric ink as shown in photo. Heat–set stamped image.

3. Color image, using brush pens. Adhere fabric to cardstock pattern, wrapping edges to back.

4. Make pleat in top front of tie. Cut and fold thin strip of scrap stamped muslin to create loose tie. Fold end to point.

5. Assemble card. Stamp image on envelope flap with fabric ink and heat–set.

Uncle Card

❧Stamp image on precut square of cardstock with metallic ink.

❧Stamp words on front bottom half of card with multipurpose ink.

❧Tear square of colored paper slightly larger than precut square. Assemble and adhere card by layering papers as shown in photo.

Wolf Father's Day Card

1. Stamp image on cardstock with multipurpose ink.

2. Color image, using brush pens and technique for Watercoloring on page 14.

3. Cut around image in square and tear right edge. Assemble card by layering with different–sized rectangles, using double–sided tape.

4. Adhere strip of cardstock to bottom of card with glue pen. Stamp words above strip with multipurpose ink.

Brother's Fishing Creel Card

⮞Stamp words on bottom front of card and stamp image on cardstock with multipurpose ink. Color image on cardstock, using brush pens and technique for Watercoloring on page 14.

⮞Cut small square around image on cardstock. Mount image on larger square of cardstock. Assemble and adhere card by layering papers as shown in photo.

Salmon Card

1. Stamp and emboss one image on linen cardstock with pigment ink and embossing powder.

2. Color image, using brush pens and technique for Watercoloring on page 14. Cut out image.

3. Stamp and emboss one image on flecked cardstock with embossing ink and powder. Cut out image.

4. Stamp one image on recycled card with dye–based ink. Cut out image.

5. Emboss select portions of image with embossing pen and powder. Stamp image on recycled card with embossing ink.

6. Cut into rectangle and mount to inside of card. Cut three rectangles in graduating sizes from recycled paper. Tear edges of smallest rectangle.

7. Assemble card by layering papers. Attach image to card with both double–sided tape and double–sided foam tape; over-lapping. Attach fishing fly.

For My Son Card

⮞Stamp words in top right corner on card with multipurpose ink. Stamp row of images down strip of cardstock with multipurpose ink.

⮞Tear and cut graduating strips and small squares of handmade paper. Assemble and adhere card by layering papers as shown in photo.

⮞Attach fishing fly to card, and adhere satin cording to left side of image strip.

Fishing Fly Squares Card

⮞Gather two identical cards. Measure and mark 1" squares on one card. Stamp images in each square with multipurpose ink.

⮞Color images, using brush pens. Cut out squares. Attach handmade paper to front of second card with double–side tape. Adhere stamped squares to handmade paper as shown in photo.

Gift for Grandfather

1. Stamp image for prepurchased wood box on precut rectangle of cardstock with multipurpose ink. Color image, using brush pens and technique for Watercoloring on page 14.

2. Attach image to slightly larger rectangle of cardstock with double–sided tape. Cut graduating squares of marbled and metallic paper. Assemble and attach layers of paper on top of box with double–sided tape as shown in photo.

3. Stamp and emboss image for gift tag on precut rectangle of cardstock with pigment ink and powder. Color image, using brush pens.

4. Cut slightly larger rectangle of metallic paper. Attach image to metallic paper with double–sided tape.

5. Punch hole in upper left corner. Tie twine around box threading through hole in tag. Tie bow.

Salmon Fly Journal

1. Stamp image on cardstock with different colors of pigment ink dabbed onto stamp. Let dry.

2. Color image, using brush pens. Tear out stamped image.

3. Wrap handmade paper around appropriate–sized piece of chipboard, securing paper to back side of board with double–sided tape. Adhere stamped image to front of board.

4. Cut three different colored handmade papers into graduating–sized rectangles. Assemble and adhere layers of handmade paper to front of journal, with stamped image on top.

5. Tie wooden charms together with raffia and adhere to front of journal as shown in photo.

Wedding

Small Box & Tag

1. Randomly stamp images on entire sheet of tissue paper with home decor ink. Let dry.

2. Cut stamped paper slightly larger than bottom and lid of box, allowing excess for tacking ends.

3. Spray adhesive on back of paper and wrap around box and lid, tacking ends inside.

4. Stamp and emboss image on cardstock with embossing ink and powder.

5. Cut around image to create tag. Punch hole. Adhere ribbon bow to box lid.

6. Thread cord through hole in tag and attach to bow.

Medium Box & Tag

1. Randomly stamp images on entire sheet of tissue paper with home decor ink. Let dry.

2. Cut stamped paper slightly larger than bottom and lid of box, allowing excess for tacking ends. Spray adhesive on back of paper and wrap around box and lid, tacking ends inside.

3. Stamp and emboss image on paper. Tear around image and adhere onto cardstock to create tag. Punch hole. Wrap ribbon around box. Tie into bow.

4. Thread cord through tag and attach to bow.

Large Box & Tag

1. Randomly emboss images on handmade paper with embossing ink and powder.

2. Cut pieces of stamped paper slightly larger than bottom and lid of box, allowing excess for tacking ends. Spray adhesive on back of paper and wrap around box and lid, tacking ends inside.

3. Stamp image on paper. Tear around image and dip edges into home decor ink. Punch hole in corner. Wrap ribbon around box and tie into bow.

4. Thread cord through tag and attach to bow.

74

Découpage Wedding Plate

1. Stamp image on cardstock with home decor ink Cut out.

2. Stamp images on underside of glass plate with home decor ink, using technique for Stamping on Glass, Ceramics & Porcelain on pages 20–21. Let dry.

3. Do not stamp words on bottom of plate because they will appear backwards. Stamp images on assorted torn papers with home decor ink.

4. Adhere papers to underside of plate with découpage medium, overlapping papers as needed. Trim excess paper from rim. Let dry.

Wedding Bells Toasting Glasses

Stamp glasses, using technique for Stamping on Candles on page 21. Stamp name and date below image, repeating technique. Let dry.

If desired, a stamp with the bride and groom's name and wedding date can be used to personal-ize. Check with a local print shop or stationery store to have one made.

Apply clear varnish or sealer to protect.

Wedding Bells Beverage Napkins

Stamp images on napkins with home decor ink as shown in photo.

If desired, a stamp with the bride and groom's name and wedding date can be used to personalize. Check with a local print shop or stationery store to have one made.

Hand–carved Rose Frame

❧Paint wood frame with acrylic paint, using a sponge brush. Let dry.

❧Randomly stamp images around frame and edges with home decor ink. Let dry.

❧Paint inside edge of frame with home decor ink, using a sponge brush. Apply sealer to protect.

Fleur–de–lis Wedding Album

1. Carefully tear handmade paper to fit front of album, leaving ½" edge. Stamp and emboss image in four corners of torn handmade paper with embossing ink and powder.

2. Lightly spray back of handmade paper with spray adhesive and adhere to cover. Cut and cover piece of cardboard with tissue. Center and adhere cardboard to top of handmade paper.

3. Cut another piece of cardboard slightly smaller than first piece. Cut piece of fabric large enough to cover cardboard, leaving enough excess to wrap around to back. Stamp image on fabric with home decor ink. Let dry.

4. Spray adhesive on back of fabric and wrap over cardboard, tacking edges to back. Trim fabric–wrapped board with various widths and lengths of ribbon, taping ends of ribbons to back.

5. Adhere charm to center of fabric board. Adhere fabric board to tissue board.

76

Gold Amor Mirror

•Make certain selected mirror is free of dirt and grease before beginning.

•Stamp mirror with home decor ink, using technique for Stamping on Glass, Ceramics & Porcelain on pages 20–21.

•Carefully lift stamp and check design. If mistake is made, immediately wipe off ink with baby wipe. Let dry. Reapply.

Large Rose Keepsakes Box

•Remove brass label holder from purchased box. Cut fabric pieces large enough to cover top and bottom of box. Stamp images on fabric for top of box with home decor ink.

•Adhere plain fabric to box bottom and stamped fabric to box top with spray adhesive. Stamp images on two short and one long piece of ribbon with home decor ink. Let dry.

•Adhere ribbons to box with spray adhesive. Reattach brass label holder to box front, slipping label inside of holder.

White Velvet Bridal Handbag

❧Purchase handbag pattern. Cut velvet, following pattern instructions. Randomly stamp images on velvet, using technique for Stamping on Velvet on page 20.

❧Assemble bag, following pattern instructions. Tie sheer ribbon bow and stitch to front of bag. Stitch pearl heart button to center of bow.

Mr. & Mrs. Edward Derbish
invite you to share their joy
in the marriage of their daughter
Beth Ann Derbish
to
Edd Gary Clark
Saturday, April thirtieth
Nineteen hundred and ninety-four
at ten thirty in the morning
Open Door Christian Church
Petaluma

Reception immediately following
Sonoma Rose Garden
Sonoma, California

Ms. Cynthia Elmore

Champagne Invitation
🍂Stamp and emboss images on front of card with embossing ink and silver pearl powder.

🍂Cut piece of cardstock slightly larger than invitation. Assemble layers of paper with invitation on top. Adhere ribbon bow to top of invitation.

Champagne Place Card
🍂Fold cardstock to form small place card. Stamp and emboss images on front of place card with embossing ink and silver pearl powder.

🍂Adhere printed name strip to front of place card. Adhere ribbon bow above printed name.

Champagne Cube Favor Box
🍂Assemble cube box as described in Cube Box Instructions on page 29.

🍂Stamp and emboss images on outside of box with embossing ink and silver pearl powder.

🍂Stuff box with mints or other desired goodies. Tie ribbon around box and into bow on top.

Champagne Photo Wedding Party Gift
🍂Stamp and emboss images on front of card with embossing ink and silver pearl powder.

🍂Trim edges diagonally with ribbon and adhere bow to upper ribbon trim. Center and adhere photograph to inside of card, visible through frame window.

Champagne Pillow Favor Box
🍂Assemble pillow box as described in Small & Large Pillow Box Instructions on page 28.

🍂Stamp and emboss images on outside of box with embossing ink and silver pearl powder.

🍂Stuff box with mints or other desired goodies. Wrap ribbon around box and adhere end of ribbon to back. Adhere ribbon bow to ribbon on box top as shown in photo.

Champagne Heart Favor Box
🍂Assemble heart box as described in Heart Box Instructions on page 80.

🍂Stamp and emboss images on outside of box with embossing ink and silver pearl powder.

🍂Stuff box with mints or other desired goodies. Adhere ribbon to edge of box lid, and ribbon bow to box top.

Heart Box Instructions

1. Lightly trace all lines from pattern onto back of cardboard or paper, using a sharp pencil and transfer paper. The dashed lines indicate where to fold.

2. Carefully cut out the box, using scissors or a craft knife and a metal straight edge. Lightly score and crease all fold lines to make the box easier to fold.

3. Turn box over. Stamp images and decorate, using brush pens, glitters, embossing powders, and inks. Let dry.

4. To assemble box, crease long band at center fold line and place crease at top of heart in center where curves meet. Fold small triangles and large tab down to the outside back of the heart; adhere.

5. Adhere small tab to inside of long band. Adhere flat heart to back side of box, covering triangles and large tab.

6. Repeat instructions to make box lid.

80

Heart Box Pattern

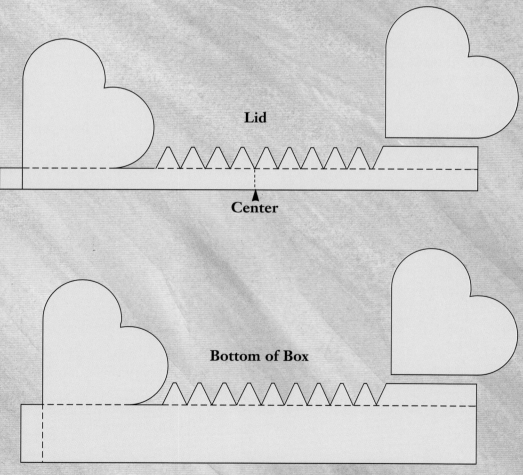

Lid

Center

Bottom of Box

Enlarge pattern 170%

Loving Heart Unity Candle

❧Ink stamp with home decor ink. Gently rest stamp on scrap paper to remove excess ink. Turn stamp over and lay flat, rubber side up.

❧Carefully roll candle over stamp, pressing down lightly to ensure even image, using technique for Stamping on Candles on page 21. Let dry.

❧Randomly dot pearlized liquid drops on candle, dotting in small sections at a time to avoid smearing drops.

Rose Candle

1. Stamp and emboss images on colored tissue paper with embossing ink and powder.

2. Tear white tissue and stamped tissue into strips. Adhere torn strips to center of candle with spray adhesive.

3. Stamp images on ribbon with home decor ink.

4. Wrap ribbon around candle and tie into bow.

50th Wedding Anniversary Card

❧Stamp image on 3"–wide sheer ribbon with home decor ink.

❧Attach stamped ribbon to front inside of photo frame card with tape. Adhere foil borders and corner embellishments to front of card with spray adhesive.

Congratulations Card

❧Cut out center of doily card. Weave cord through doily and secure ends on back of card.

❧Stamp image on vellum paper with home decor ink. Trim edges of vellum paper and adhere to back of doily card. Center image to appear through cut out. Adhere bow to front of card.

25th Anniversary Doily Card

1. Carefully cut out scalloped frame from doily notecard, using craft knife, and set aside. Mount a rectangle of metallic cardstock to underside front of doily notecard.

2. Tear a piece of handmade paper into a rectangle. Stamp and emboss image on torn handmade paper with embossing ink and powder. Attach stamped image to front of card, using double–sided tape.

3. Adhere cut–out scalloped frame back over top of stamped handmade paper. Wrap sheer ribbon around front fold of card and tie into bow.

4. Stamp and emboss image on matching envelope flap with tinted embossing ink and powder.

Dove Card

❧Stamp and emboss images on precut card with embossing ink and metallic powder. Sprinkle powders over selected areas of stamped images, overlapping slightly.

❧Emboss card edges with powder, using straight edge and embossing pen. Embellish dove images with sparkle glue. Assemble and adhere card by layering papers on front of second card as shown in photo.

Now & Forever Card

1. Stamp and emboss words on front of oval photo frame card with embossing ink and pearl powder.

2. Stamp image on sheer ribbon. Attach image to inside front of card with double–sided tape.

3. Wrap two pieces of ribbon diagonally around front of card and secure to inside with double–sided tape. Adhere small bow to top ribbon, and charm to bottom ribbon on front of card as shown in photo.

4. Cut front of second oval photo frame card and adhere to inside of card, covering rough edges of ribbons.

Housewarming

Paper Maché Bowl

🍂Tear several strips of handmade and tissue papers.

🍂Stamp and emboss images on strips with home decor ink, pigment ink, and embossing powder.

🍂Soak strips in paper maché paste and wrap around a bowl. Let dry. Paint rim with home decor ink.

Peas Address Book

1. Stamp images on cardstock with multi-purpose ink and heat–set. Color images, using brush pens and technique for Watercoloring on page 14.

2. Tear around image. Stamp and emboss words on cardstock with em-bossing ink and powder.

3. Tear around image and paint edges, using brush pen. Wrap mul-berry paper around address book and adhere with spray adhesive. Tack ends inside.

4. Assemble and adhere layers of paper on front of address book as shown in photo. Tie ribbon bows around front fold of book.

Veggie Apron

☙Stamp images on separate muslin fabric square with multipurpose ink and heat–set.

☙Color images, using fabric markers, and heat–set again.

☙Sew seam binding around fabric square onto purchased apron. Sew seam binding around edges of entire apron, leaving two long strips for apron ties.

Veggie Pot Holder

1. Cut out two fabric pieces according to purchased pattern instructions. Stamp images on one fabric piece with multipurpose ink and heat–set.

2. Color images, using fabric markers, and heat–set again.

3. Dip sponge in same ink and spatter between images. Heat–set.

4. Place batting between two fabric pieces. Sew diagonal lines on fabric pieces spacing 1½" apart in grid pattern, using sewing machine. Sew binding around edges and add loop for hanging.

Veggie Tea Towel

☙Stamp images on fabric strip with multipurpose ink and heat–set.

☙Color images, using fabric markers, and heat–set again.

☙Sew stamped strip to top and bottom of towel with seam binding, wrapping end of binding around back of towel on each side.

Veggie Oven Mitt

1. Cut out four fabric pieces according to purchased pattern instructions. Stamp images on two fabric pieces with multipurpose ink and heat–set.

2. Color images, using fabric markers, and heat–set again. Dip sponge in same ink and spatter between images. Heat–set.

3. Place batting between one stamped and one plain fabric piece. Sew diagonal lines on fabric pieces spacing 1½" apart in grid pattern, using sewing machine.

4. Repeat batting and diagonal sewing instructions, creating two quilted pieces. With right sides together, sew mitt together. Turn mitt right side out and sew binding around bottom edge and add loop for hanging.

85

Veggie Recipe Box

1. Paint box with home decor ink. Paint rectangle on top of lid with home decor ink. Lightly dab ink around bottom edge of box, using foam brush, to create grass.

2. Carefully stamp images on lid with home decor ink. Stamp images on sides of box with home decor ink. Color images, using fabric pens.

3. Mask off ½" strip around edge of lid, using masking tape. Sponge small squares around lid with home decor ink, using piece of sponge, leaving space between each square.

4. Stamp images in spaces between squares with home decor ink.

5. Paint thin line around top and bottom edges of masked off area with home decor ink.

6. Stamp enclosure cards to match images on box with pigment ink as shown in photo.

Grape Tapestry Bowl

1. Select a flat, unglazed bowl, and plan to use kiln at a ceramic studio.

2. Sponge glaze color around rim of bowl. Paint glaze on image, using sponge brush. Carefully stamp rim.

3. Stamp images in center of bowl with glaze as shown in photo.

4. Finish bowl with clear glaze and bake in kiln.

Porcelain Coaster Set

1. Stamp images on porcelain squares with multipurpose ink. Paint images with low–fire porcelain paints, blending colors, using technique for Blending on page 14. Bake in kiln.

2. Paint coaster edges with home decor ink, using a sponge brush. Cut black felt into squares slightly smaller than coaster size and adhere to bottom of coasters.

3. Stamp image on cardstock with multipurpose ink. Color image, using brush pens, and cut out in a square.

4. Assemble layers of paper on top of box as shown in photo. Line box with tissue paper and place coasters inside.

Open House Invitation

❧Stamp image on card with metallic ink. Stamp message over previous image with multipurpose ink.

Colonial Home Invitation

❧Stamp images on separate pieces of cardstock with multipurpose ink. Color images, using brush pens.

❧Cut house image into square. Assemble and adhere invitation by layering papers as shown in photo.

Pennsylvania Stone House Card

❧Emboss image on card with black pigment ink and embossing powder.

❧Color images, using brush pens and technique for Watercoloring on page 14. Lightly add color to deckle–edge of card, using brush pen.

❧Cut window flaps on all windows, using a craft knife. Fold as shown in photo.

Connecticut Valley House Card

❧Stamp and emboss images on card with pigment ink and embossing powder.

❧Color images, using brush pens.

❧Cut and fold doors of house image as shown in photo, using a craft knife. Adhere ribbon to card.

Colonial Gift Wrap

1. Stamp and emboss images on newsprint sheets with pigment ink and embossing powder. Stamp images on newsprint with dye–based inks.

2. Color images, using brush pens.

3. Mask images, using technique for Masking technique on page 18. Stamp word images over masked images with dye–based ink, entirely covering newsprint.

4. Wrap gift and tie with ribbon.

We've Moved Card

Stamp image on card with multipurpose ink. Color image, using brush pens and technique for Watercoloring on page 14.

Garden Party

Garden Party Lights

1. Lightly trace Cube Box Pattern on page 29 onto back side of vellum paper and cut out.

2. Stamp images on outside of box with home decor ink. Let dry.

3. Color images, using brush pens. Let dry. Repeat above steps for desired number of lights.

4. Fold and assemble boxes, re–enforcing tabs and flaps with glue. Before gluing top, place tape on underside of lid and cut small "X" through tape and vellum.

5. Insert light bulb through cut in top of box. Place piece of tape over wire to secure.

Floral Garden Luminary

1. Randomly stamp images on vellum paper with home decor ink. Color images, using brush pens. Let dry.

2. Make a bag, using Making a Bag technique on page 27.

3. Cut top of bag to desired height, using deckle–edged scissors.

4. Turn bag upside down and dip edges in home decor ink. Let dry.

5. Fill bottom of bag with sand and place glass votive with candle in bag to create luminary.

Please join us

Garden Party Place Mat

1. Purchase desired number of place mats and one extra mat for practice. Wash mats to remove sizing and iron dry.

2. Stamp images on paper and color with textile paints.

3. Cut out images. Arrange cut out images in desired design to form border strip. Cut away parts of paper images laying outside of border.

4. Tape images into place on place mat with double–sided tape to use as a stamping guide. Experiment on extra place mat to determine proper consistency of paint to be used for stamping. Too much thinning will blur image, and paint which is too thick will blob on place mat.

5. Load paint on stamp and avoid filling up the wells of stamp, using the side of a #5 or #6 watercolor paintbrush. Work quickly to avoid drying.

6. Stamp images on place mat. Heat–set.

7. Fill in images with very diluted wash of textile paint. To avoid bleeding, do not overload brush or stroke on too much color. It is best to fill in color from center of area. Observe how paint spreads and brush on more if needed. Have heat tool handy to dry spreading color if necessary.

8. When satisfied with results of experiment, stamp on actual place mats. Cover center of place mat with clear self–adhesive shelf paper, leaving border exposed for stamping. It is helpful to use stamp positioner to assure proper duplication of design.

9. Stamp images on entire place mat border with textile paints. Touch up broken lines, using a #1 paintbrush.

10. When stamping is complete, remove center mask. Heat–set.

11. Paint images with textile paints. Heat–set. Weave ribbon around inner edge of border to finish place mats.

12. Sew ribbon ends with invisible thread to secure in place on back.

Garden Party Napkin Ring

❧Create reverse mold, using technique for Working with Modeling Compounds on pages 22–23. Press modeling compound into mold, then peel away. Place flat and cut around image. Remove excess clay and smooth edges.

❧Roll out a pencil–sized cylinder of clay, using your hands. Flatten slightly. Twist from ends to create 7" spiral. Wrap spiral around paper cylinder and press ends together, flattening slightly. Carefully press clay image over fastened ends. Leave clay on cylinder, bake, and cool.

❧Paint with acrylic paints and seal with acrylic varnish or clear gloss glaze.

Garden Party Napkin

❧Purchase desired number of napkins to match place mats and one extra napkin for practice.

❧Stamp images on paper to create design for two opposite corners of napkins. Stamp image once, then mask and stamp image again to create three–imaged design, using technique for Masking on page

18. When pleased with design, stamp same imagery on two opposite napkin corners with textile paint, using same techniques as on place mat. Touch up lines where needed. Heat–set.

❧Brush on color wash. Heat–set. Weave ribbon in corner and tie small bow, securing ribbon ends with invisible thread.

Garden Party Invitation & Envelope

1. Stamp and emboss image on handmade paper with embossing ink and powder. Tear around image.

2. Color image, using brush pens. Color word portion of stamp, using brush pen and technique for Coloring & Painting on the Stamp on page 14.

3. Stamp on bottom of card. Edge front bottom of card, using same brush pen. Stamp and emboss image on translucent paper with embossing ink and powder. Cut around image to size of inside flap and attach with double–sided tape.

4. Assemble and adhere card by layering papers as shown in photo.

5. Color stamp, using brush pens, and stamp image on front left side of envelope.

6. Color image, using brush pens, and technique for Watercoloring on page 14.

91

Garden Invitation

❧Stamp images on cardstock with multipurpose ink. Color stamp, using brush pens and technique for Coloring & Painting on the Stamp on page 14.

❧Tear around invitation image and adhere to inside of card. Draw squares on piece of cardstock, using brush pen and straight edge. Adhere cardstock to card. Wrap twine around fold of card and tie into bow.

Cotswold Porcelain Card

❧Stamp image on porcelain bisque square with multipurpose ink. Let dry.

❧Paint image and edge of square with porcelain paints. Adhere paper, ribbon bow, dried flowers, and porcelain image to card as shown in photo.

Garden Party Invitation

❧Adhere square of paper to card. Stamp images on paper with multipurpose ink as shown in photo.

❧Color stamp, using brush pens and technique for Coloring & Painting on the Stamp on page 14.

Baby Girl's Birth Announcement

1. Cut oval out of center of card. Stamp images on top of card with dye–based ink.

2. Stamp and emboss image at bottom of card with embossing ink and powder.

93

3. Stamp and emboss images onto strips of paper with embossing ink and powder, cutting to fit sides of oval on front of card as shown in photo.

4. Adhere strips to card. Adhere foil embellishments and bow. Adhere photograph to inside of card.

Iridescent Ball Ornament

1. Remove cap from iridescent ball ornament.

2. Swirl two colors of acrylic paint inside ball. Turn over and let remaining paint drain into paper cup. Let dry.

3. Randomly stamp image all over ball with home decor ink. Replace cap and adhere trim.

4. Tie wire–edge ribbon into bow and adhere to ornament.

Bunny Bib

⊱Paint images with fabric inks and technique for Coloring & Painting on the Stamp on page 14.

⊱Stamp image in center of bib, using technique for Blending on page 14. Heat–set.

⊱Paint images and border with fabric inks, using technique for Watercoloring on page 14. Heat–set.

Baby Shower Invitation

⊱Stamp images on colored paper with small amount of bleach.

⊱Paint edges of letters, using brush pen to create shadow effect. Stamp ribbon, using brush pen and technique for Coloring & Painting on the Stamp on page 14.

⊱Adhere ribbon ends to inside front of card with tape. Adhere cardstock liner to inside of card. Adhere bow to front of card.

Christening Card

⊱Stamp and emboss image on linen cardstock with embossing ink and powder. Color image, using brush pens and technique for Watercoloring on page 14.

⊱Stamp and emboss images on front of photo frame card. Emboss edge of oval with embossing pen.

⊱Adhere watercolored image to inside of card. Adhere bow to front top of card.

Ducky Gift Wrap

⊱Randomly stamp and emboss images on wrapping paper with embossing ink and powder. Color images, using brush pens.

⊱Wrap gift. Tie ribbons into bow. Adhere bow and charm to top of gift.

Baby's Handprint Card

1. Roll out modeling compound and flatten into a 2½" circle. Stamp image into clay circle. Poke small hole through clay image at top with toothpick. Bake in oven following manufacturer's instructions. Let cool.

2. Paint clay image with home decor ink. Stamp and emboss images on card with pigment ink and pearlized powder. Spray with matte spray fixative to protect.

3. Tear and cut textured papers into squares larger than clay image. Assemble paper squares on front of card as shown in photo.

4. Thread ribbon through hole in clay image and tie into bow. Adhere clay image to center front of card.

Rubber Ducky Frame

1. Cut 2" square window in center of 5"x 7" foam core, using craft knife and metal straight edge. Place frame on top of white paper and trace around outside and inside as a guide, using a pencil.

2. Randomly stamp images on paper with home decor ink. Draw vertical lines on stamped paper ¼" apart, using straight edge and metallic pen.

3. Color stripes, using brush pen. Do not draw over stamped images. Color images, using brush pens and technique for Watercoloring on page 14.

4. Spray back of paper with adhesive and attach to frame, wrapping excess paper to back. Cut an "X" inside frame window and fold triangular flaps to back of frame. Cut ½"–wide strip of white paper and adhere to inside of window with spray adhesive.

5. Cut piece of mat board to cover back of frame and adhere with spray adhesive. Attach self–adhesive easel to back of frame.

Halloween

Halloween Luminary

1. Stamp and emboss translucent vellum paper with multipurpose ink and embossing powder. Color images, using brush pens. Highlight images with sparkle glue.

2. Color background, using brush pen and technique for Watercoloring on page 14.

3. Rub pearlized powder over entire bag and spray with fixative. Make paper into a bag, using technique for Making a Bag on page 27.

4. Cut top edge of bag, using decorative scissors. Color top edge of bag with permanent ink, using straight edge.

Haunted Mansion Card

☙Stamp and emboss image on white paper with pigment ink and clear powder. Stamp and emboss image on inside of card with pigment ink and clear powder. Color image, using brush pens.

☙Stamp image on scratch paper with any type ink and cut out image to create mask. Lay mask over stamped and colored image. Sponge raised dye inks over mask around stamped image, using a cosmetic sponge.

☙Adhere white paper to pretorn construction paper with glue pen. Assemble and adhere card as shown in photo.

Spook Door Card

☙Stamp and emboss image on precut and torn recycled paper with pigment ink and clear powder.

☙Color image, using brush pens. Stamp image two times on colored paper with pigment ink.

☙Cut out images. Attach images to recycled paper with foam tape. Assemble card by layering as shown in photo.

Treat Bag

1. Stamp images on cardstock by coloring top portion of stamp with multipurpose ink, and candy with pigment ink. Heat–dry. Color images, using brush pens.

2. Highlight image with sparkle glue. Stamp images on cardstock with pigment ink. Let dry.

3. Color images, using brush pen. Cut out images. Cut rectangular shape from glossy paper and glue to bag. Tear first image from cardstock and adhere to glossy paper. Adhere cut images to bag.

4. Tie raffia into bundle and adhere to upper corner of bag.

Halloween Lollipop Cover

1. Stamp and emboss image on 8" white fabric with fabric ink and sparkle powder. Heat–set.

2. Wrap fabric over lollipop and tie with ribbon.

3. For embroidered cover, stamp image on colored fabric square with fabric ink and embroider over image with embroidery floss. Sew decorative stitch around edges of fabric square.

4. Wrap fabric over lollipop and tie with colored twine.

BOO!

TRICK or TREAT

You're invited
Time 7 PM
Date October 31
Place 13 Spooky Ln.
Phone 668-6399
R.S.V.P.

Boo! Card

❧Stamp and emboss image on pretorn construction paper with embossing ink and powder. Stamp images on recycled and torn construction paper with dye–based ink.

❧Punch two small holes in card and tie cord through holes. Run line of glue along edge of card with glue pen, then emboss with tinsel powder.

❧Adhere images to card with glue pen. Adhere trinkets to card with craft glue.

Witch's Hat Card

❧Stamp image on cardstock with multipurpose ink. Color image, using brush pens.

❧Tear edges around stamped image. Tear various colored papers in graduating sizes. Assemble and adhere card by layering papers as shown in photo. Attach trinket with craft glue.

Halloween Pin

❧Roll out clay modeling compound to ⅛" thickness, using technique for Working with Modeling Compounds on pages 22-23. Stamp image into clay for pin. Cut image from clay, using craft knife, and smooth edges with fingers. Bake following manufacturer's instructions.

❧Paint pin with acrylic paints. Cut rectangle window in center of card. Adhere colored cardstock inside of card.

❧Randomly stamp images on front of card with pigment ink. Adhere pin to back of pin. Attach pin inside of card.

Pumpkin Graveyard Scene Invitation

❧Brayer cardstock, using technique for Brayering on page 25. Repeat several times until paper is desired color. Let dry.

❧Stamp image on colored cardstock. Tear around stamped image and adhere to corrugated paper. Stamp image four times on cardstock. Tear sides of cardstock.

❧Stamp image on speckled handmade paper, tear sides, and adhere to previously stamped cardstock. Adhere corrugated paper to top of handmade paper.

Pumpkin Votive

1. Roll out clay modeling compound to ¼" thickness, using technique for Working with Modeling Compounds on pages 22-23. Stamp image into clay. Cut out stamped image, using craft knife.

2. Cut out circle of clay slightly larger than base of votive. Wrap votive with double thickness of aluminum foil.

3. Mold clay image around foil on votive to shape. Slide foil and clay image carefully off votive to retain tubular shape. Bake according to manufactuer's instructions.

4. Paint with acrylic paint. Adhere clay image to clay base with silicone adhesive.

99

Halloween Popcorn Ball Cover

❧Stamp and emboss image on butcher paper with embossing ink and powder. Color image, using brush pens.

❧Cut image into rectangle, using decorative scissors. Color edges of paper, using brush pen and straight edge.

❧Wrap paper around popcorn ball. Tie with colored twine.

Witchy Mask

1. Stamp image on glossy paper with multipurpose ink by masking bottom portion of stamp. Stamp additional images around first image with multipurpose ink.

2. Color images, using fabric markers. Cut out images with bottom cut in shape of bat head.

3. Trace Witchy Mask Pattern onto glossy paper and cut out. Adhere images to mask. Highlight images with sparkle glue. Let dry.

4. Adhere colored raffia to back of mask. Cover dowel with construction paper to match color of raffia. Hot–glue dowel to back right side of mask.

Spider Mask

1. Trace Spider Mask Pattern onto felt and cut out. Draw web pattern on mask with sparkle glue. Let dry.

2. Stamp and emboss images on construction paper with embossing ink and powder. Cut out images. Attach image to mask with thread. Attach other image to mask with double–adhesive foam tape.

3. Adhere construction paper to back of mask for support. Cut out eyes. Paint dowel. Draw web pattern on dowel with glitter glue. Let dry.

4. Pin ribbon streamers to top of dowel. Hot–glue dowel to back left side of mask.

Witchy Mask Pattern

Spider Mask Pattern

Enlarge patterns 175%

Thanksgiving

Colonial Wreath

🍂Stamp and emboss images on card with embossing ink and powder. Color image, using brush pens.

🍂Cut front flap vertically, using deckle–edged scissors. Emboss deckle–edge with embossing pen.

🍂Punch top left side of card. Thread ribbon through holes and tie bow.

Harvest Wagon Card

🍂Stamp and emboss image on cardstock with pigment ink and powder. Color image, using brush pens. Tear around image.

🍂Adhere image to front of card. Add twine bow.

Cornucopia Invitation

🍂Stamp and emboss image on cardstock with pigment ink and embossing powder. Color image, using brush pens.

🍂Stamp and emboss words below first image with embossing ink and powder. Cut out larger rectangle of colored paper and tear edges.

🍂Assemble cardstock, ribbon, and colored paper as shown in photo.

Maple Leaves Card

❧Stamp image on precut paper with pigment ink. Cut handmade paper slightly shorter and wider than stamped paper. Assemble and adhere layers of paper as shown in photo.

❧Tie twigs together with raffia and attach charm with cord to twigs. Adhere twigs and charm to front of card.

Tumbling Leaves Invitation

❧Randomly stamp images on front of frame card with home decor ink. Color images, using brush pens.

❧Adhere ribbon to inside of card so it appears inside window. Stamp image on vellum and center inside of card. Adhere edges of card together.

Turkey Card

❧Stamp and emboss image on cardstock with pigment ink and embossing powder. Color images, using brush pens. Cut out.

❧Adhere feathers to back of image. Assemble and adhere image and layers of colored deckle–edged paper on card as shown in photo.

Velvet–wrapped Centerpiece Candle

❧Measure circumference and height of candle. Cut velvet to make sleeve for candle, using measurements. Stamp images onto velvet with fabric paint, using technique for Stamping on Velvet on page 20. Match colors on velvet to color of table runner.

❧Sew side seam of sleeve and blind–stitch hem at top and bottom. Slip sleeve over candle. If desired, wrap candle with contrasting ribbon at edges of sleeve.

❧Tie ribbon bow around center of candle as shown in photo.

Thanksgiving Table Runner

❧Stamp images on scrap paper, cut out images, and lay out design on fabric with double–sided tape. Use as stamping guide.

❧Apply fabric paint to stamps, using a sponge brush. Mask stamps as needed to achieve desired design. Let dry; heat–set.

❧Line runner with desired fabric, sew tassel to point, and topstitch edges.

Oak Spray Place Card

❧Stamp image on cardstock with multipurpose ink and color, using brush pens. Score and fold card. Cut through both layers of card around edge of image.

❧Add powdered pigment edging, with glue pen. Adhere contrasting colored cardstock to inside of card and trim showing slight edge. Write name.

Gobbler Place Card

❧Stamp and emboss image on cardstock with pigment ink and embossing powder. Color image, using brush pens.

❧Score a crease horizontally avoiding stamped image. Cut around top of image above score lines. Fold card in half.

❧Emboss bottom edge of front flap with glue pen. Color remaining edges of front, using brush pen. Adhere feathers to back of front flap. Write name.

Leaves Place Card

1. Roll out modeling compound to ⅛" thickness. Stamp image in clay and cut out each leaf. Smooth edges of images.

2. Roll out ½" x 1½" log of clay and slightly flatten sides. Cut lengthwise slit halfway through top center of log, wide enough for card to slip into.

3. Slip scrap card into slit and bake pieces according to manufacturer's instructions. Let cool and remove scrap card.

4. Rub various pigment powders on leaves and base. Brush pieces with clear gloss glaze. Let dry.

5. Adhere leaves to base with silicone adhesive. Stamp and emboss image on card with embossing ink and powder. Emboss edges with embossing pen and powder.

6. Adhere card to torn colored paper. Slip place card into holder as shown in photo.

Tumbling Leaves Place Card

❧Randomly stamp images on prefolded card with home decor ink. Color images, using brush pens.

❧Adhere printed name strip onto center of ribbon. Wrap twig with cord. Adhere twig and name to card as shown in photo.

Christmas

Wooden Bird Ornament

1. Stamp image onto basswood with permanent ink. Let dry.

2. Cut around image, using a scroll saw. Drill a hole at top and sand edges.

3. Paint image with translucent paints. Spray with sealer.

4. Thread cord through hole and knot ends.

Ho Ho Ho Card

1. Stamp image on precut craft paper with multi-purpose ink and heat–set.

2. Stamp images on recycled card with multi-purpose ink.

3. Color images, using brush pens and technique for Watercoloring on page 14.

4. Attach precut stamped paper to front of card with double–sided tape.

Santa's Hat Gift Wrap

❧Stamp and emboss alternating rows of images on paper with embossing ink and powder. Color images, using brush pen.

❧Add pearlized liquid drops to image, using paintbrush. Wrap gift with paper and tie with satin–edged ribbon as shown in photo.

Garden Santa Card

1. Stamp image on card-stock with multipurpose ink and heat–set.

2. Color image, using brush pens and technique for Watercoloring on page 14.

3. Fold colored paper in half and cut slightly larger than precut imaged paper. Tie ribbon around folded edge, thread bells on ribbon, and tie small bow on outside.

4. Assemble and adhere paper layers as shown in photo. Stamp image on bottom center of card with pigment ink. Let dry.

Santa Card

1. Stamp image on cardstock with multipurpose ink. Heat–set.

2. Color image, using brush pens and technique for Watercoloring on page 14.

3. Tear around image. Adhere image to inside of photo frame card.

4. Emboss inside edge and around outside window edge with glue pen and embossing powder.

5. Tie ribbon into bow around fold of card.

Christmas Quilt Card

▰Stamp and emboss image on card with embossing ink and powder. Cut out image.

▰Color image, using brush pens. Assemble and adhere card by layering paper as shown in photo.

▰Punch hole through top center of card and tie with ribbon bow and cord.

Poinsettia Cut–out Card

1. Open card. Stamp and emboss image on inside left with embossing ink and detail powder.

2. Color image, using brush pens and technique for Watercoloring on page 14.

3. Score vertical line about halfway through left side of card. Do not score over image, just score at top and bottom.

4. Cut out around right side of image, stopping at scored line. Fold card to make sure it works.

5. Stamp image on metallic paper with home decor ink.

6. Stamp words with multipurpose ink.

7. Adhere metallic paper to inside right of card.

8. Emboss line down left side of card, using emboss-ing pen and powder. Tear right edge of metallic paper.

Cardinal Pop–up Card

1. Stamp image on cardstock with multipurpose ink and heat–set.

2. Cut around image on left side and score in half. Stamp and emboss image in upper right corner with embossing ink and powder. Emboss edge with glue pen and embossing powder.

3. Stamp second piece of cardstock with images. Color images, using brush pens and technique for Watercoloring on page 14.

4. Cut around images. Score in half. Then score "V"–shaped lines in center of card and crease as shown in photo. Fold handmade cardstock for card.

5. Emboss left edge of card with glue pen and embossing powder. Stamp image with home decor ink on front and inside left top corner of card.

6. Assemble and adhere layers inside card.

Folk Angel Ornament

🍂Roll out piece of modeling compound to ⅛" thickness, using technique for Working with Modeling Compounds on pages 22-23. Stamp image into clay and cut out. Smooth edges with fingers. Poke hole in top of ornament. Bake ornament according to manufacturer's instructions. Let cool.

🍂Paint ornament with acrylic paints. Thread ribbon through hole and knot near ends.

108

Little Christmas Tree Card

🍂Stamp image on precut cardstock with multi-purpose ink. Color image, using brush pens. Apply liquid appliqué to bottom of image. Let dry; heat–set.

🍂Cut down card. Cut a window large enough for image to show though in front of card, using a craft knife and a metal straight edge. Draw border around edge of window, using brush pen.

🍂Adhere image to inside of card with double–sided tape, centering image through window. Punch two small holes near folded edge of card. Thread piece of twine through holes and tie into bow.

Porcelain Bear Ornament

🍂Stamp image on porcelain ornament with home decor ink. Let dry.

🍂Paint image with low–fire porcelain paints. Sponge low–fire porcelain paint around edges. Bake according to manufacturer's instructions.

🍂Thread ribbon through hole and tie ends into a bow.

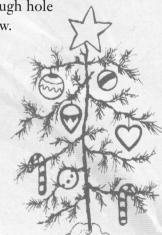

Let It Snow Card

🍃Stamp and emboss image on cardstock with pigment ink and powder. Color image, using brush pens and technique for Watercoloring on page 14.

🍃Paint snow portion of image with liquid applique. When dry, puff liquid applique, using heat tool.

🍃Cut around image. Cut colored paper slightly larger than image. Adhere image to paper. Cut window same size as image in front of handmade card. Center and adhere mounted image to inside of card, visible through window.

Snowman Ornament

🍃Stamp onto porcelain bisque ornament with home decor ink.

🍃Paint image with low–fire porcelain paints. Bake according to manufacturer's instructions. Thread cord through hole and knot ends.

Santa's Cookie Plate

1. Measure diameter of center circle and outer edge of clear glass plate. Recreate shape of plate by lightly drawing concentric circles of same dimensions onto lightweight handmade paper, using a compass. This is your stamping guide.

2. Cut out and discard center circle. Cut around outside circle, leaving ½" excess paper all around. Erase any pencil lines.

3. Stamp images with home decor ink onto ring of paper, using stamp positioner.

4. Paint images with acrylic paints, using fine–tip paintbrush Let dry.

5. Apply découpage medium to bottom edge of plate. Press stamped paper into medium, smoothing out wrinkles and bubbles. Let dry.

6. Trim excess paper from outer edge. Apply two additional layers of découpage medium over paper. Let dry.

7. Clean excess découpage from center of plate with wet paper towel. Paint outer edge of plate with acrylic paint. Let dry.

Santa's Tumbler

❧Stamp images on glass tumbler with home decor ink, using technique for Stamping on Candles on page 21. Let dry.

❧Paint images with low–fire porcelain paints, using fine–tip paintbrush. Bake according to manufacturer's instructions.

Holly Leaf Votive

🍂Stamp images on rim of glass votive with home decor ink. Trim with sparkle glue. Let dry.

🍂Place top of votive upside down on top of ink pad and twist votive to apply ink to edge. Let dry.

🍂Pour wax granules inside votive, add wick, and light.

Angel Votive

🍂Trace votive circumference on handmade paper and cut out, leaving ½" excess. Trace votive bottom on paper and cut out.

🍂Stamp and emboss images on cutout strip with embossing ink and powder.

🍂Adhere stamped paper to sides of votive with spray adhesive. Wrap rough ends to bottom and adhere bottom cut out to bottom of votive. Adhere trim to top edge.

The Holly Votive

🍂Stamp images on votive upside down with home decor ink. Place top of votive on top of ink pad and twist votive to apply ink to edge. Let dry.

🍂Tie ribbon around bottom of votive and secure.

Cardinal Ornament

1. Stamp image on paper with multipurpose ink. Color image, using brush pens and technique for Watercoloring on page 14.

2. Center glass square over image and trace around outer edge of glass. Cut along traced edge and around edges of image.

3. Stamp partial image on glass with home decor ink. Place image between two pieces of glass and attach with tape.

4. Paint tape with mixture of gold and black home decor ink to create antique look.

5. Thread cord through holes in glass. Tie ribbon into bows, and adhere to ornament with adhesive.

Pine Cone Wreath Gift Box

❧Stamp and emboss image on precut cardstock with pigment ink and powder. Color image, using brush pens.

❧Cut colored and handmade paper in graduating sizes to fit on top of box.

❧Tie ribbon bow around box lid and assemble and adhere papers by layering on top of box as shown in photo.

Stack of Christmas Boxes

1. Stamp and emboss images on colored paper with embossing ink and tinsel powder.

2. Draw lines on paper, with marker. Highlight images with sparkle glue. Wrap large box.

3. Stamp and emboss images on metallic paper with pigment ink and powder. Heat–set.

4. Highlight images with sparkle glue. Wrap medium box.

5. Stamp and emboss images on colored paper with embossing ink and tinsel powder. Highlight images with sparkle glue. Wrap small box.

6. Tie stack together with wire–edge ribbon. Stamp and emboss image on tag with embossing ink and tinsel powder.

7. Write name, using embossing pen and tinsel powder. Punch hole in corner of tag. Thread ribbon tail through hole in card and tie ribbon into bow.

Stack of Soaps

🍂Stamp image on tissue paper and ribbon with home decor ink.

🍂Wrap soaps in tissue paper. Tie ribbons around stack of wrapped soaps and create decorative bow on top.

Christmas Bulb House

1. Trace Birdhouse Patterns on page 59 onto cardstock. Cut out.

2. Stamp images on house, using technique for Coloring & Painting on the Stamp on page 14.

3. Cut and assemble house and make shingled roof from handmade paper as instructed on page 58.

4. Apply liquid appliqué to shingles and let dry overnight.

5. When dry, puff up liquid appliqué, using heat tool. Sprinkle glitter on top.

6. Color stamps, using brush pens. Stamp images on cardstock and cut out.

7. Adhere images around edges of roof. Adhere roof to house. Tie ribbon into loop and attach to top of roof for ornament hanger.

Gingerbread Birdhouse

1. Stamp and emboss image on cardstock with embossing ink and tapestry powder. Color image, using brush pens. Cut out.

2. Stamp and emboss image three times on cardstock with pigment ink and powder. Color images, using brush pens. Cut out.

3. Trace Birdhouse Patterns on page 59 onto cardstock. Cut out.

4. Cut and assemble house as instructed on page 58. Adhere first image to front of house. Adhere cut out images to house with glue pen. Trace roof pattern onto handmade paper.

5. Stamp and emboss image repeatedly with pig-

ment ink and powder to form pattern as shown in photo.

6. Cut strips of construction paper, using scallop–edged scissors. Adhere straight edges of strips to top of roof and eaves. Adhere roof to house.

7. Trace chimney pattern on construction paper. Use strip of cardstock to wrap around top of chimney. Adhere one image to chimney, then adhere chimney to roof.

8. Apply liquid appliqué to entire house for icing. Let dry overnight.

9. When dry, puff using heat tool. Adhere ribbon loop to inside of chimney for ornament hanger.

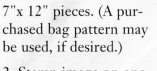

Red Velvet Bag

1. Cut velvet into two 7"x 12" pieces. (A purchased bag pattern may be used, if desired.)

2. Stamp image on one piece of velvet with home decor ink, using technique for Stamping on Velvet on page 20.

3. Assemble bag by placing wrong sides together and sewing sides and bottom. Leave a ½" gap 4½" from top on each side of bag. Turn bag right side out.

4. Fold top 3" down inside bag. To form casing for ties, sew around top edge of bag, 1½" from top. Sew around bag again, 2" from top.

5. Thread cord through casings and tie. Stuff bag with wide sheer ribbon.

Velvet Wine Bag

1. Cut velvet into an 11" x 16" rectangle. Trace bottom of wine bottle on wrong side of velvet, using pencil. Cut out, leaving margin for seam allowance.

2. Randomly stamp images on velvet with home decor ink, using technique for Stamping on Velvet on page 20. Stamp some images with no ink.

3. Sew long ends of rectangle together, with right sides together, then sew bottom circle. Turn right side out. Fold in top of bag and blind–stitch hem inside.

4. Put bottle inside bag and tie with tasseled rope. Measurements and amount of velvet needed vary depending on size of bottle.

To make any of the following stockings, purchase desired stocking pattern and cut fabric pieces according to instructions. Test inked stamp on scrap fabric until satisfied with images. Then decorate as follows.

Blue Crown Stocking

1. Randomly stamp images on cut fabric with home decor ink. Cut oval from contrasting fabric 1" larger on all sides than image to be stamped on fabric. Stamp image in center of oval with home decor ink.

2. Assemble stocking, following pattern instructions.

3. Handstitch oval to front of stocking, then stitch braided cord over edge of oval.

4. Tie ribbon into bows and stitch to front of stocking.

Red Holly Stocking

❧ Stamp images on fabric with home decor ink, spacing rows 1" apart as shown in photo. Stitch ⅜"–wide satin ribbon between each row of stamped images.

❧ Assemble stocking, following pattern instructions.

❧ Tie ribbon into bows and handstitch to corner of stocking. Tie jingle bells onto ribbon ends.

White Angel Stocking

❧ Randomly stamp images on cut fabric with home decor ink.

❧ Assemble stocking, following pattern instructions.

❧ Tie ribbon into bows and handstitch to front of stocking. Adhere charm to center of bow.

Angel Ornament

1. Roll out piece of paper modeling compound into a 2¼" x 3" oval for ornament, using technique for Working with Modeling Compounds on pages 22-23. Let dry.

2. Stamp image into clay with multi-purpose ink. While ink is still wet, gently dab on pigment powder, using small, dry paintbrush. Carefully brush away excess powder.

3. Spray ornament with matte sealer.

4. Mix pigment powder with liquid glue. Brush a border around edge of oval, using a paintbrush. Let dry.

5. Tie two ribbons together in a bow and adhere charm to center of bow. Adhere ribbon tails to ornament.

Angel Limoges

1. Select a flat limoges, and plan to use kiln at a ceramic studio.

2. Apply glaze to stamp, using a sponge brush.

3. Stamp image on center of lid. Reglaze stamp, then slowly roll sides of box over stamp.

4. Paint edges with accent color as shown in photo. Finish box and lid with clear glaze and bake in kiln.

Santa Ornament

1. Stamp image onto fabric with fabric ink and heat–set.

2. Paint image with fabric paints and heat–set.

3. Embellish with glitter glue and liquid appliqué. Let dry overnight.

4. Puff up liquid appliqué, using heat tool. Cut out image, leaving ¾" border around edges. Cut piece of fabric into same shape and cut out image.

5. Sew fabrics together, with right sides together, leaving space to turn right side out. Turn right side out, stuff, and stitch space closed.

6. Adhere cord around edge, making a loop at top for hanger.

Spruce Trees Gift Wrap

🍂Stamp images on tissue paper with multipurpose ink. Make lighter impressions by not re–inking stamp in between stampings. Heat–set.

🍂Stamp image over first images with metallic ink. Wrap gift with stamped tissue and ribbon bows, adding a sprig of artificial berries to bow.

Red Snowflake Present

🍂Stamp and emboss images on colored paper with embossing ink and two colors of sparkle powder.

🍂Wrap gift. Stamp images on satin ribbon with home decor ink. Tie ribbon around gift and attach sheer wire–edge ribbon bow to top.

Green Stamped Gift Bag

❧Stamp and emboss images on gift bag and tissue paper with embossing ink and powder.

❧Stuff bag with tissue and gift. Twist star garland around bag handles.

Noel Gift Wrap

❧Stamp images on colored paper with metallic ink. Let dry.

❧Wrap gift in stamped paper and tie with ribbon bow.

Green Stamped Ribbon Gift

❧Stamp images on ribbon with home decor ink.

❧Wrap gift and tie ribbon around gift.

Snowflake Ornament

🍂Remove cap from ball ornament. Stuff inside of ornament with desired color of shredded mylar and replace cap.

🍂Randomly stamp image all over ball with home decor ink. Let dry.

🍂Adhere trim. Thread ribbon through top of cap and tie ends into a bow.

120

Small Holly Ornament

1. Remove cap from ball ornament and pour gold leaf adhesive size into ball. Swirl ball until entire inside is covered. Turn over and let remaining size drain into small paper cup. Adhesive size will dry completely clear.

2. Pour pigment powder inside ball. Swirl ball until entire inside is covered. Turn ball over to tap out excess.

3. Randomly stamp image all over ball with home decor ink.

4. Embellish with glitter glue when dry.

5. Replace cap and adhere trim. Thread ribbon through top of cap and tie into a bow.

Poinsettia Gift Box

🍂Stamp and emboss image on box with embossing ink and powder.

🍂Color images with embossing pens and emboss with powder.

🍂Tie ribbon into bow around box as shown in photo.

Paper Ornament

1. Stamp and emboss 20 images on cardstock with embossing ink and powder. Cut out images.

2. Color images with embossing pens. Emboss with powder, leaving five images partially uncolored.

3. Add pearlized liquid drops to images and let dry.

4. Cut 2" equilateral triangle out of scrap matboard. Score and crease sides of each piece, using triangle as guide.

5. Assemble two domes out of five images. Match sides and adhere. Before last piece of each dome is adhered, secure tassel to the inside with tape so that tassel protrudes out of center of dome.

6. Secure loop in similar fashion at center of other dome. Let dry.

7. Assemble a strip of 10 images to form center portion of ornament. Use partially uncolored pieces for top portion of strip. Let dry.

8. Attach two domes to the center strip. Let dry. Thread top loop through a gold bead.

Small Pillow Box

❧Trace Small Pillow Box Pattern on page 28 onto wrong side of cardstock. Cut out and score.

❧Turn cardstock over to stamp and emboss images with embossing ink and powder. Let dry.

❧Assemble box, securing ends with tape. Wrap cord around box and tie into bow.

Small Pixie Pillow Box

❧Trace Small Pillow Box Pattern on page 28 onto wrong side of cardstock. Cut out and score.

❧Turn paper over and randomly stamp images with metallic and dye–based inks. Let dry.

❧Assemble box, securing ends with tape. Tie bullion around box.

Hanukkah Pillow Box

❧Trace Large Pillow Box Pattern on page 28 onto wrong side of cardstock. Cut out and score.

❧Turn paper over and randomly stamp images with metallic ink. Let dry.

❧Assemble box, securing ends with tape. Wrap ribbon around box and tie into bow.

Shalom Card

1. Stamp image on cardstock with pigment ink for image, and using brush pen for letters. Emboss entire image with clear embossing powder.

2. Cut image into square, tearing top and bottom edges. Emboss all edges with embossing pen and powder.

3. Randomly stamp images on blue cardstock with embossing ink and powder. Tear handmade paper into square slightly larger than stamped square.

4. Assemble and adhere card by layering papers as shown in photo. Wrap cord around front of card twice, secure with knot, and attach charm.

Jerusalem Card

1. Stamp image on colored paper with pigment ink. Heat–set.

2. Tear image into square. Embellish with glitter glue. Let dry.

3. Stamp images on card with metallic ink. Let dry.

4. Cut out square of white cardstock larger than stamped square. Emboss edges with embossing pen and powder.

5. Tear white handmade paper into rectangle larger than square. Tear square of white cardstock larger than cutout square.

6. Cover torn square completely with home decor ink, using a cosmetic sponge. Let dry.

7. Adhere sheer ribbon to front of card. Assemble and adhere card by layering papers as shown in photo.

Shalom Cube Box

1. Make a cube box, following Cube Box Instructions on page 29.

2. Ink stamp, using pigment ink for image, and using brush pen for letters. Stamp six images on cardstock. Emboss with clear powder.

3. Cut images into squares of equal size. Emboss edge of each square with embossing pen and powder.

4. Adhere images to all sides of box. Tie box with sheer ribbon bow and bullion. Tie a loop of bullion around bow knot to secure charm.

Chai & Star Gift

1. Randomly stamp images on vellum with two metallic inks. Spray with fixative.

2. Wrap gift with colored paper, then wrap with vellum. Stamp images on ribbon with metallic ink. Let dry.

3. Wrap stamped ribbon around gift and tie into bow.

4. Stamp and emboss image on cardstock with embossing ink and powder. Cut out.

5. Adhere to metallic cardstock. Cut and fold cardstock to make small tag. Punch hole in corner and thread cord through hole and around bow, knotting cord to secure tag to bow.

Driedel Card

1. Stamp and emboss image on colored cardstock with embossing ink and powder. Embellish with glitter glue.

2. Stamp and emboss two images on front of card in upper left corner and lower right corner with embossing ink and powder.

3. Color images, using brush pens. Draw thin squiggles from each image with glitter glue. Let dry.

4. Lightly sponge small cardstock rectangle with home decor ink, using a cosmetic sponge. Let dry.

5. Emboss edges, with an embossing pen and powder. Assemble and adhere card by layering papers as shown in photo.

Dove Petite Notecard & Envelope

1. Stamp image on bottom left side of card and on flap of envelope with multipurpose ink, using technique for Masking on page 18. Heat–set.

2. Color image, using brush pen.

3. Draw cloud on scrap paper and cut out for pattern. Trace cloud onto envelope flap, then cut out so flap looks like cloud.

4. Lightly sponge bottom of flap with dye–based ink, using technique for Sponging on page 26. Sponge cloud shapes on card with dye–based ink.

5. Cut a window in card. Stamp image inside card with multipurpose ink, so image is visible through window. Heat–set.

6. Color image, using brush pens. Embellish card and envelope with glitter glue.

Menorah Card

1. Stamp image on colored folded paper with dye–based and home decor inks. Let dry.

2. Stamp and emboss images on cardstock with embossing ink and powder. Color large image, using brush pens.

3. Cut large colored image into rectangle and cut out small image. Cut rectangle out of center of folded paper to create window. Center colored image on inside front of card so image is visible through window.

4. Attach small image to upper left corner of card with double–sided foam tape. Wrap cord around front of card twice and tie bow at top of card.

PSX stamp numbers/names used in this book.

Pg 33–F1724 Morning Glories
F1981 Kind Words
G1553 Feel Special
G2005 Summer Butterfly Border
K1299 Lilac Bot.
Pg 34–D2238 Brushed Leaf
F1899 Curly Line Heart
F1982 Love Will Find a Way
K2222 Heart Frame w/Roses
K2230 Forever in the Heart
G1242 Calligraphy Invitation
G1694 Filigree Heart
Pg 35–B1933 Sun Symbol Sm.
F1117 Rose Bot. Alphabet
F1610 Celebrate
F1817 I Miss You
G1853 How Much
G1932 Sun Symbol Lg.
K1775 Right Acanthus
K2134 Heritage Roses
Pg 36–B2271 Brushed Rose Bud
E2266 Brushed Thanks!
G1611 Script Congratulations
G2228 Teapot w/ Roses
K2291 Four Brushed Roses
Pg 38–B1662 Sm. Starfish
E1529 Lagoon Triggerfish
F1145 Lighthouse
F1661 Lg. Starfish
F1817 I Miss You
Pg 39–B2013 Florentine/A
B2014 Florentine/B
B2015 Florentine/C
F1817 I Miss You
K1556 Magnolia
Pg 40–F1769 Zuni Indian Pot
F1928 Small Goat
F1930 Small Deer
K1796 Navajo Serape
SK147 Petroglyphs Set
Pg 41–A2282 Brushed Bumblebee
E1629 Single Magnolia
E2266 Brushed Thanks!
F1234 Using Deepest Sympathy
G2235 Brushed Rose I
SK144 Floral Silhouettes Set
Pg 42–E1240 I Love You
F270 Happy Anniversary
F2014 Florentine/B
K040 Bearded Iris
K1636 Hybrid Rose Bot.
K2047 Morning Glory
K2209 Honeysuckle
K2253 Nasturtium
Pg 43–F1899 Curly Line Heart
F2230 Forever in the Heart
K2227 Brushed Roses & Leaves
Pg 44–B1329 Sweet Rosebuds

F2246 Be Mine Valentine
G1242 Calligraphy Invitation
K1414 Lg. Heart Quilt
K2221 Clematis/Jasmine Heart
G1694 Filigree Heart
Pg 45–B2270 Brushed X & O
C2237 Swirl Heart
F2230 Forever in the Heart
G1897 Three Hearts
K2222 Heart Frame w/Roses
PI105 Sweetheart Pixie Set
Pg 46–B2017 Florentine/E
B2024 Florentine/L
B2027 Florentine/O
B2034 Florentine/V
B2269 Brush Heart
F1984 Captured My Heart
G1897 Three Hearts
K1643 Heart of Hearts
P1105 Sweetheart Pixie Set
Pg 47–C1647 Tulip Stencil
C2236 Sm. Brushed Rose
D2238 Brushed Leaf
F318 Wonderful Birthday
G2235 Brushed Rose I
K2291 Four Brushed Roses
Pg 48–F318 Wonderful
   Birthday
PI 102 Birthday Pixie Set
Pg 49–A412 Plain Heart
A2273 Brushed Star
B009 Small Bear Paw
B997 Calico Bear Sm.
B2268 Brushed Bow
C2267 Brushed Balloon
D2039 It's a Party
E154 Happy Birthday Cake
E749 Bear Family
E1972 Fuzzy Honey
F568 Patches
F569 Ben
F1977 To/From Bear
F2320 Brushed Happy Birthday
G1174 Fuzzy Bear
K1421 Have a Heart Teddy
K1911 Back to Back Bears
PI105 Sweetheart Pixie Set
SK108 Teddy Bear Set
Pg 51–F1724 Morning Glories
K2047 Morning Glory
Pg 52–K1778 Four Women
Pg 53–E1935 Med. Spiral
F1924 Square Spiral
F2320 Brushed Happy Birthday
K1778 Four Women
Pg 54–E1526 Quaking
   Aspen Leaf
F1772 Sun Print
F2320 Brushed Happy Birthday
G1669 Aspect to the Sun

K1827 Satin Bow
PI102 Birthday Pixie
Pg 55–B1185 Magnolia
B1354 Twin Roses
F1724 Morning Glories
G1180 Old Fashioned Rose
G2004 Rambling Rose
G2006 Field Poppy
G2207 Fuchsia Hummingbird
K023 Cabbage Rose
K774 Pansy Bot.
K1468 Hydrangea Bot.
K1628 Long Stem Bouquet
K1637 Peach Bot.
K1695 Bucket of Tulips
K2048 Queen Anne's Lace
K2135 Windmill
K2138 Rhododendron Hall
Pg 56–B564 Floral Egg
B1731 Honey Bee
C623 Doily Egg
C1647 Tulip Stencil
D259 Easter Egg
D1225 Hearts Entwined
D1391 Amor
F1203 Fabergé Easter Egg
F2011 Ruffled Iris
F2105 Lavender Spray
F2165 Gardenia
G553 Vine & Rose Heart
G1180 Old Fashioned Rose
G1242 Calligraphy Invitation
G1251 Ivy Heart
G1821 All My Love
G1889 Remember Moments
K1636 Hybrid Rose Bot.
K1696 Calla Lily Bot.
K2152 Primula Bot.
Pg 57–A1307 Petite Sunflower
B176 Cherub w/ Basket
B1329 Sweet Rosebuds
B1354 Twin Roses
D1225 Hearts Entwined
E1991 Sunflower Corner
K2183 Feather Medley
Pg 60–B564 Floral Egg
D259 Easter Egg
D685 Bunny Border
F1919 Spring Chicks
PI103 Garden Set
PI104 Celebrations Set
Pg 61–B564 Floral Egg
D1944 Tiny Cabbage Teapot
F1918 Easter's on Its Way
K1943 Bunny Tea
SK111 Easter Rubber Set
Pg 63–K2047 Morning Glory
Pg 64–C1743 Tapestry
   Rose Leaf
D1744 Tapestry Rose Leaflets

D1745 Tapestry Rosebuds
F1724 Morning Glories
F1736 Tapestry Rose Lg.
Pg 65–C2203 Star Flower
F1833 Special Grandmother
F2048 Queen Anne's Lace
G2005 Summer Butterfly
Pg 66–B2233 Brushed Rose &
   Leaves
C2205 Tea Cup Border
D022 Watering Can
D1350 Wedgewood Teapot
E2076 Wonderful Aunt
F1724 Morning Glories
SK307 Garden Set
Pg 67–A279 Corner
B1354 Twin Roses
D670 Double Roses
K1636 Hybrid Rose Bot.
Pg 68–D1697 Cottonwood
   Leaf
F1143 Oak Leaf
K1457 Black Walnut Tree
K1501 Winter Tree
Pg 69–K2145 Marsh Wren
Pg 70–F267 Happy Father's Day
F1772 Sun Print
F2068 For My Father
F2075 Wonderful Uncle
G1855 Wolf
SK147 Petroglyphs Set
Pg 71–E2070 For My Son
F2071 For My Brother
G1635 Hook, Line & Sinker
G1653 Coho Salmon
G1654 Fishing Creel
SK322 Fly Fishing Set
Pg 72–G1313 Wood Duck
D1604 Classic Salmon Fly
F1832 Special Grandfather
Pg 73–B030 Lace Bow
B1721 Stencil
F012 Happy Wedding Day
F395 Gift Tag
F2093 Now & Forever
G1748 Hand-carved Rose
Pg 74–D1330 Rose Corner Spray
F012 Happy Wedding Day
F384 Bouquet Bells
F1019 Rose Shower
Pg 75–B1764 Fleur-de-lis Sm.
G1748 Hand-carved Rose
K1791 Left Acanthus
Pg 76–B2233 Sm. Brushed
   Rose & Leaves
D1391 Amor
K2227 Brushed Rose & Leaves
Pg 77–G1748 Hand-carved
   Rose
Pg 79–B1721 Stencil

125

Sources

126

Index

Metric Conversion

Inches	MM	CM	Inches	MM	CM	Inches	CM	Inches	CM	Inches	CM
⅛	3	0.9	2	51	5.1	10	25.4	21	53.3	32	81.3
¼	6	0.6	2½	64	6.4	11	27.9	22	55.9	33	83.8
⅜	10	1.0	3	76	7.6	12	30.5	23	58.4	34	86.4
½	13	1.3	3½	89	8.9	13	33.0	24	61.0	35	88.9
⅝	16	1.6	4	102	10.2	14	35.6	25	63.5	36	91.4
¾	19	1.9	4½	114	11.4	15	38.1	26	66.0	37	94.0
⅞	22	2.2	5	127	12.7	16	40.6	27	68.6	38	96.5
1	25	2.5	6	152	15.2	17	43.2	28	71.1	39	101.6
1¼	32	3.2	7	178	17.8	18	45.7	29	73.7	40	104.1
1½	38	3.8	8	203	20.3	19	48.3	30	76.2	41	106.7
1¾	44	4.4	9	229	22.9	20	50.8	31	78.7	42	109.2